PERCEPTUAL-MOTOR BEHAVIOR
AND EDUCATIONAL PROCESSES

Second Printing

PERCEPTUAL-MOTOR BEHAVIOR AND EDUCATIONAL PROCESSES

By

BRYANT J. CRATTY

Associate Professor and Director
Perceptual-Motor Learning Laboratory
University of California
Los Angeles, California

With a Foreword by

Leon Whitsell, M.D.

University of California Medical School
San Francisco, California

CHARLES C THOMAS • PUBLISHER

Springfield • Illinois • U.S.A.

Published and Distributed Throughout the World by

CHARLES C THOMAS•PUBLISHER

Bannerstone House

301-327 East Lawrence Avenue, Springfield, Illinois, U.S.A.

Natchez Plantation House

735 North Atlantic Boulevard, Fort Lauderdale, Florida, U.S.A.

© 1969. *by* CHARLES C THOMAS•PUBLISHER

Library of Congress Catalog Card Number: 68-18290

With THOMAS BOOKS *careful attention is given to all details of manufacturing
and design. It is the Publisher's desire to present books that are satisfactory as
to their physical qualities and artistic possibilities and appropriate for their
particular use.* THOMAS BOOKS *will be true to those laws of quality that assure
a good name and good will.*

First Edition, First Printing, 1969
First Edition, Second Printing, 1970

Printed in the United States of America

FF-17

FOREWORD

DURING the past decade there has been increasing concern in this country over the large number of children with learning problems. These disorders include not only the severe forms of generalized mental subnormality, but also the much larger groups of children handicapped by various borderline conditions, particularly the specific learning disabilities.

Recently these specific learning disabilities have been more or less officially classified among the manifestations of "minimal brain dysfunction" in a study sponsored by the National Institute of Neurological Diseases and Blindness. The inclusion of numerous patterns of intellectual, perceptual, conceptual, linguistic, and sensory-motor difficulties within this same general category creates some confusion about the diagnosis.

Additional uncertainty frequently develops over the question of whether any lesion—anatomical or chemical—actually exists. And in every case, the relative importance of environmental forces and psychological factors in shaping the basic disorder must be critically considered.

Although it carries the implication of a relatively minor, hidden type of difficulty, the term *minimal brain dysfunction* is often misleading. In contrast to the terms *minimal brain damage* or *brain injury*, which were formerly applied to the same type of problem, this newer designation implies flexibility, remediability—a generally favorable prognosis.

However, the actual handicap of a child so diagnosed often is far from minimal because of its disastrous impact on the child's total development, particularly if remedial help is too long delayed. Or, if its potential harmfulness is ignored by those dealing with it, misdiagnosis of this type of trouble can be extremely dangerous for the child and his family.

The inherent diagnostic difficulties, inadequate understanding, deficiencies in our educational systems, and limited resources for evaluational and remedial help have all seriously complicated these problems. Increasingly urgent demands by parents for help have unwittingly fostered the premature development of various experimental or even ill-advised forms of treatment.

Among these debatable methods, a number of "motor treatment" programs have been widely publicized recently as panaceas for specific learning disabilities, speech and language disorders, and hyperkinetic behavior. A large number of children with these conditions, have already been placed in such treatment programs. While physical training programs will generally improve physical fitness and motor skills, there is no proof that such training will help other types of learning problems.

The potential harmfulness in the indiscriminate use of certain motor treatments for some individual children and their families must be recognized, inasmuch as there is general agreement that any type of treatment should have direct relevance to the specific needs of the child. Nevertheless, even the more dubious "motor therapies" derive a certain superficial credibility from the common concurrence of motor and perceptual-motor problems with other specific learning disabilities.

Early motor difficulties, especially those in the gross coordination categories, often lead to progressive exclusion by peer groups from play activities, adding social maladjustment to the child's personal burden. Lack of remedial help and insufficient opportunity for practice of motor skills tend to aggravate developmental deficiencies in a downward spiral.

Unhappily for many children with developmental lags and other borderline motor handicaps, very few American school systems have any formal physical education programs until the level of junior high school or beyond, aside from "playground activities" carried out by regular classroom teachers.

At the present time only limited consideration is usually given by either physicians or educators to the need for earlier and more carefully planned physical education programs in the schools. Often the major efforts of physical educators appear to be directed toward the development of future star athletes and pennant winning teams. Clumsy and poorly trained children and those with medical prescriptions for limited participation in physical education are often subjected to ridicule and may be assigned to serve as locker room attendants or sent to a study hall.

In a majority of school systems no organized programs for corrective or remedial physical education are available, in spite of clear evidence showing that serious deficits in physical development and fitness exist in an enormous number of young people and adults in the United States.

Professor Cratty has had an extensive practical background as a teacher in physical education at all levels. His original research has involved studies of perception and physical development in the education of the blind, mentally retarded, and neurologically impaired. For several years he has provided vigorous leadership in a movement toward urgently needed changes in attitudes toward physical education programs.

Having developed an unusually broad grasp of the relationships between his own studies and recent research in the neighboring fields of medicine, psychology, and sociology, he expresses concern over the proper use of physical education and simultaneously cautions against claiming too much for movement activities in education.

In this book the publishers are making more generally available a selection of Professor Cratty's timely lectures and essays on interrelated topics. These papers include provocative discussions of social acceptance, body image, gender identification, and other aspects of personality development in relation to perceptual-motor and educational processes.

Although originally prepared for presentation to educators, these papers provide a needed series of discussions and critical reviews which will also be valuable to physicians and others in the paramedical fields dealing with children. There is a serious need for more effective communication among our various cooperating professions. This book is a solid contribution to this end.

Leon J. Whitsell

PREFACE

AT TIMES educators have fragmented the human personality into several parts when attempting to elicit
behavioral changes within the classroom. In schools
during the Middle Ages, the mental, spiritual and physical
were assigned to discrete niches, and little overlapping
was perceived to occur. Beginning with the Renaissance,
however, some pedagogues began to examine the human
being's potentials for action as avenues through which to
improve the intellect.

During recent years in the United States, the pendulum
seems at times to have swung even further and claims
for the curative powers of perceptual-motor, sensori-
tonic, or similar programs abound. But as with all
pendulums, it probably will begin to swing in the other
direction again.

The materials presented within the pages of this
text are an attempt to prevent the "lash-back" which
could occur if educators find that the promises of the
proponents of some of the various movement panaceas
are not fulfilled. The author has tried within recent
years to focus the scrutiny of the scientific method of
problem solving upon the role of perceptual-motor
activities in the total educational setting. It is felt that
movement tasks may play an increasingly larger role in
the total educative process, but at the same time should
not be viewed as the manner in which all children's
cognitive development may be enhanced, and certainly
not the only method by which more severe deficiencies
of atypical children can be corrected.

The various chapters within the text are reprints of
speeches and articles directed to physical educators
and educators. When confronting the former, the author

usually pleads for a more thorough statement of claims, substantiated by experimental evidence, and when addressing the latter, the writer argues for time in which to pursue longitudinal studies of behavioral change which may be elicited in normal and atypical children as a function of various kinds of perceptual-motor training; and at the same time suggests that the educators consider available data which advocate that incorporating certain perceptual-motor tasks within the educational setting will elicit positive results.

More and more school administrators scrutinize the evidence of the researcher before embarking upon program change. It has been attempted in the pages which follow, when possible, to document carefully the claims made for and against the role of motor activities within the programs of general and special education. It is believed that as new evidence is forthcoming, these kinds of activities may play an increasingly important role within the schools of our country.

Much of the material contained in these pages has been derived from the writer's research which has been sponsored by the National Science Foundation, the National Institute of Neurological Diseases and Blindness, a Special Donor's Grant, and the Los Angeles County Mental Retardation Services Board. Other materials have been summarized from the author's texts, including *Movement Behavior and Motor Learning, Social Dimensions of Physical Activity, Developmental Sequences of Perceptual-Motor Tasks, and Psychology and Physical Activity.*

The initial portion of this text deals with perceptual-motor functioning with a context encompassing the total human personality. It has been attempted to outline how one might consider the causes of action patterns and how movement behavior and human intelligence overlap.

The second section treats the manner in which movement behavior interacts with some of the components of classroom functioning and with the ways in which children may organize their environment in intelligent ways.

The concluding section deals specifically with how one

may incorporate movement activities into programs for children with learning difficulties because of various deficits in their visual-motor systems. Training methodologies for the blind, the orthopedically handicapped, the neurologically impaired, as well as the retarded are found in this final portion of the book.

The attempt is made to encourage teachers to observe and consider the obvious when they educate children—how they move. Additionally, it is hoped that meaningful operational and theoretical guidelines are presented which will aid educators to modify the perceptual-motor behavior of children into important tools with which to shape their total personality.

Bryant J. Cratty

CONTENTS

SECTION II

SPECIAL EDUCATION

A. General Considerations

B. Blind Children and Youth

C. The Clumsy Child Syndrome

D. The Mentally Retarded

E. The Orthopedically Handicapped

Appendix

PERCEPTUAL-MOTOR BEHAVIOR
AND EDUCATIONAL PROCESSES

SECTION I

PERCEPTUAL-MOTOR BEHAVIOR AND EDUCATION

A. Movement and the Human Personality

Chapter 1

MOVEMENT AND THE INTELLECT

WITHIN RECENT years educators have shown an increased interest in exploring the role of perceptual-motor activities within the total educational program. This interest has been spurred by national publicity based upon theoretical speculations by certain clinicians working with atypical children (11) as well as by data emanating from the laboratories in which research with youngsters is being conducted.

Historically, one is able to trace the emergence of several philosophical viewpoints regarding the relationships of physical activities to the total educational program. At one extreme are opinions prevalent during the Middle Ages which completely divorced physical functioning from mental and spiritual goals. It was believed that the body was immoral and, thus, interest in action and attempts to improve bodily functioning in sports and games was the work of the Devil and should be avoided.

Renaissance man adopted a more liberal outlook. Physical activity was, at times, accorded a reasonably respectable role within learning environments. While some accorded vigorous activity a place in educational programs only because of its apparent use in drawing off excess energies which might interfere with intellectual functioning, others adopted a naturalistic approach to the education of the child and moved physical activity into a more central position within the school

Speech to Principals, Los Angeles City Schools, April 1967.

(30). Many contemporary educators traveling further across the scale view physical activity as an important learning modality meeting basic physiological needs, as well as more subtle psychosocial ones revolving around positive self-acceptance, social interaction and similar goals of education.

Within the past ten years, however, some clinicians working with severely neurologically handicapped children through movement have published remarkable assertions regarding physical-intellectual relationships.

Through the use of sequential locomotor activities it has been claimed that the central nervous system functioning of normal youngsters may be enhanced and that such behaviors as seeing, hearing, and thinking will improve if certain simple motor tasks are practiced.

This writer is not convinced of the veracity of these latter claims; however, it is believed that there *are* relationships between the quality and quantity of obvious motor output of children and their ability and/or inclination to engage in various tasks within the classroom. It is intended in the pages which follow to explore some experimental data which support certain of these relationships and to present some of the implications of these findings for the total educational program.

It is believed that motor activities can be a helpful learning modality; but, to best utilize movement tasks within schools one must carefully examine research findings rather than simply paying blind devotion to one of the popular 'movement messiahs.''

Piaget, Kephart and others have attested to the importance of early motor learnings to the development of the intellect, basing their assertions primarily upon observation that the first kind of behavior that children evidence is motoric (23,29). However, recent experimental findings testify to the importance of early visual imprinting upon later intellectual and emotional functioning (15); while the studies by Dennis and others suggest that artificial restrictions of children's motor activities do not necessarily result in developmental lag in the motor realm (12). Dayton, Haith and others have found, for example, that infants seem capable of visually tracking objects and of fixating their attention upon things during the first few hours of their lives (10,18). The way to elicit mental retardation in a child is to restrict his visual experiences rather than to limit his movements (15).

Evidence by Held and his co-workers supports the assumption that early visual experience on the part of mammals (cats) and humans must be accompanied by movement if they are to form accurate perceptions of their world (19). The evidence of imprinting gained from the laboratories of Hess and others attest to the importance of physical effort when attempting to elicit this "wired-in" behavior, i.e. the following response in chicks (20). If one is to generalize from these findings, one might conclude that motor activity is vital to the early perceptual development of human children. However, it might also be hypothesized that the nervous systems of cats and chicks are different from those of human children; and that, indeed, infants at rather early ages, whether able to move or not, may participate vicariously in the dynamics of their environments through vision. Evidence supporting this assumption is forthcoming from the laboratories of Abercrombie and her colleagues who have presented findings that children in late childhood and early teens who have lacked movement attributes from birth (cerebral palsey) perform on an equal level on tests of intelligence and perception with normal children (1).

Kilpatrick and others have also found that illusions elicited by observing rooms whose surfaces have been modified to produce various size-distance distortions can be quickly dispelled when one examines these surfaces with a stick, or *watches* another person touch the room's surfaces with the same stick (24).

Findings of this nature suggest that the human infant handicapped by an impaired or a missing component of his sensory-motor system (i.e. movement deficits, hearing loss, blindness, etc.) can still acquire concepts through various kinds of compensatory behaviors. Thus to state that movement capacities are imperative to the formation of intelligence would seem to be an exaggeration. However, the implication that various visual-motor pairings are important channels through which normal infants form initial perceptions of their world and themselves is a truism beyond doubt.

Experimental evidence relating intelligence measures to motor ability scores can be summarized in two statements. If one holds constant the I.Q. range of the subjects and gradually makes the motor tasks more complex, a progressively higher relationship can be demonstrated between the two measures. On the other hand, if one holds constant the complexity of the motor tasks and examines the scores of children progressively lower on the intellectual scale, again, successively higher correlations will be obtained (4).

However, every educator can attest to the fact that an I.Q. measure does not always correlate directly to classroom success, problem-solving ability, creative thinking and attitudes about things intellectual. Certain measures of intellect are related to certain measures of motor ability; however, the two behaviors are not mutually inclusive. In the pages which follow, it is intended to clarify the nature of these differences as well as the manner in which the two facets of behavior sometimes overlap.

MOVEMENT ACCURACY IS NECESSARY TO EXPRESS THE INTELLECT

One of the more obvious ways in which intellect and movement capacities converge is in tasks involving the transcribing of thoughts to paper in the form of handwriting. We have worked with several children in our clinical program during the past several years whose verbal I.Q.'s are from 40 to 50 points above their performance I.Q.'s. These children evidence a considerable amount of frustration when attempting to transcribe their thoughts quickly to paper or to rapidly finish an arithmetic assignment. Their cognitive processes are average or superior, while their abilities to express their thoughts in a school assignment are inferior.

Most school tests and assignments are performed under the stress of speed; they are "power" tests, rather than simply tests of knowledge. Children with visual-motor problems have great difficulty in these kinds of situations, although they can often deliver a good speech, can perform well on a verbal test, and can otherwise give evidence of sound thought processes.

It is believed that such children can be aided through two general approaches: (a) Concrete steps should be taken to improve their visual-manual skills including tasks involving finger dexterity, hand-eye coordinations similar to writing, and tasks designed to aid them to perceive their hands and fingers; (b) Alternative methods of expression should be opened to them. They should be taught to type, even though this, at times, may be difficult for them. The "timing" attribute needed in typing may be less disrupted than the attribute underlying the more fluid movements required in handwriting. At times they should be tested verbally by the teacher, rather than being subjected to written tests under the domination of a stopwatch.

We must frequently observe and read about the importance of work methods selected for the tasks upon the performance score elicited. One of the important work methods underlying academic performance involves the ability to express the intellect through the accurate hand movements.

MOTOR TASKS CAN ELICIT OPTIMUM LEVELS
OF AROUSAL

An often-confirmed finding in the psychological literature is the fact that there are optimum levels of alertness, activation, or arousal necessary for the efficient performance of a given task. Simple tasks require higher levels of arousal, while more complex ones require less tension on the part of the performer in order to elicit best performance scores (13).

There are several kinds of investigations which indicate that this principle is operative in the performance of mental work. During the 1930's and 1940's, Courts and

Freeman (2,14) demonstrated that if levels of muscular tension were raised in individuals, i.e. by having them exert 50 per cent of their maximum pressure on a handgrip, they performed better on tasks involving the memorization of word lists and similar verbal-cognitive skills. The tension elicited from simple muscular work somehow raised their level of activation to the optimum for the performance of the mental skills required of them. The findings of these early investigations have been verified in more recent studies (13,32).

Contemporary researchers also suggest that excess tension, when *lowered* by engaging in endurance type activities, can elicit superior performance in various intellectual activities. Gutin and his colleagues at the City College of New York have elicited superior · performance in arithmetic tasks following moderate exercise on a treadmill (17). These researchers warn, however, that the best intellectual performance will be elicited only in well-trained subjects after moderate exercise, rather than in either poorly trained individuals who have been subjected to exhaustive work or highly trained subjects who similarly have been run to exhaustion. It would thus seem that moderate exercise will produce optimum reductions in excess tensions which will contribute to efficient mental work.

GAME PARTICIPATION AS REINFORCEMENT
FOR CONCEPT ACQUISITION

Another group of investigations has recently produced evidence which indicates that the privilege of participating in games will motivate children to learn better concepts related to reading and to language. Humphrey, in several studies of this nature, has demonstrated that children taught various language concepts with an "active game method" learned significantly more than the control group who was taught through the traditional medium of a language workbook.

Skills involving structural and semantic analysis,

phonics and word recognition, as well as vocabulary, were reinforced in games such as "steal the bacon" with positive results. The results and implications of these findings have been summarized in a recent text (22). Humphrey has concluded that the high motivational state elicited in game situations produces the desired results in language skill improvement.

A 1958 study by Oliver, dealing with retarded youngsters in England, also contains findings relative to reinforcement through games of traditional learnings. His experimental group of retardates participating in games several hours a day improved in various tests of intelligence to a significant degree over controls who remained in classrooms throughout the day, as is traditional. Both these experimenters urge caution when interpreting these findings, as I do. Playing ball does not contribute in a direct way to cognition; however, the indirect manner in which success, in observable and easily measurable indices of success, contributes to various components of intellectual endeavor is apparent from an inspection of these findings (28).

AIDING SELF-CONTROL AND LENGTHENING ATTENTION SPAN

It is an easy task to excite and arouse children through vigorous and active games and exercises. However, it is becoming increasingly apparent that an important manner in which perceptual-motor activities can be utilized within the educational setting is to enable the child to place himself under his own control. To learn, a child must attend to something for a period of time; he must focus and look at materials on his desk top for more than a few moments. If he is easily distracted, he cannot learn the traditional classroom tasks well. Research findings which support the possible use of motor activities to lengthen attention span are forthcoming from a recent investigation by Maccoby, who found a high correlation between scores elicited from directions like "draw a line as slowly as you can" and "walk from here to there as slowly as you can" and I.Q. scores (26).

While the data from the above experiment do not necessarily indicate that slowing a child down and aiding him to achieve degrees of motor control will *cause* an improvement in mental functioning, they do suggest future investigations which would explore this problem.

It is relatively easy to time a child's typical attention span, and we have done this in our clinical program. We have then placed such children on balance tasks in which the beam is gradually lengthened and in similar situations which required more prolonged attention to the task. In most of these cases we have measured a definite improvement in attention span to the motor tasks involved; whether this increased attention span has transferred to classroom learnings has not been determined as yet. However, it is reasonable to believe that unless a child can be encouraged to concentrate on *something* (whether a mental or motor task) for a period of time longer than he has looked at anything in the past, he cannot be expected to focus upon classroom tasks for the prolonged period of time necessary for their acquisition.

THE SATISFACTIONS GAINED IN PHYSICAL EFFORTS CONTRIBUTE TO A SUCCESS SYNDROME

It is an often-stated platitude that a child's self-concept can be enhanced through successful participation in games. However, the data supporting such a statement are often difficult to obtain. Measuring something as esoteric as "the self-concept" is difficult enough and has been criticized as too vague a term for experimental verification by several writers.

We might pose the question, however, from a negative standpoint. What will continual failure in physical endeavors do to a child's self-concept, or in more pragmatic terms, to his capacity to perform? We have recently collected data which begin to answer such a question.

A cross-sectional study of retardates of a number of classifications and chronological ages enabled us to study developmental trends in the performance scores obtained. Children within this study who were classified as "educationally handicapped" and as "educable retardates" (I.Q. 70) exhibited the best performance scores on six kinds of perceptual-motor tasks in late childhood, and after the age of twelve and thirteen began to decline in their ability to execute the activities presented to them (4).

It appeared from an inspection of this data that repeated failure to do well in games and similar experiences might have discouraged these children so that they would simply withdraw from vigorous activity and as a result begin to lose the capacity to perform well. Neurologically handicapped children, the majority of whom are boys, are informed daily in concrete terms that they are failures in activities highly valued by their peers. One wonders what adults would do if they were informed regularly that they were hopeless by their superiors as they arrived at their prized jobs.

One might ask oneself how much of a boy's or girl's self-concept is composed of his ability to perform well in games, particularly between the ages of five and seventeen years. A critical question, of course, is how much this kind of playground failure will generalize itself to a lowering of the self-concept in classroom activities. It is apparent, at times, that one of the more valued compensations engaged in by poorly performing males is withdrawal to academics. They become tense collectors of bugs, chemists, and PhD's at age ten. Some boys and girls may totally reject themselves and refuse to function at any kind of task, mental or motor because of continual rejection in motor activities highly prized by their peers.

Riding bicycles, playing games, and dancing are motor activities which signal the emergence of various developmental levels in children and adolescents. If these activities cannot be accomplished with reasonable proficiency, a chain of failure may be formed.

GROSS MOVEMENT AS A LEARNING MODALITY

When one conceives of how information and/or concepts may be transmitted to another person, it is usual to think in terms of types of sensory input. A classroom teacher may present a demonstration utilizing the visual processes, encourage tactile explorations of textures, shapes and forms, and/or present verbal information.

However, if one observes the total child in action as he moves through space, it is apparent that the sensations he depends upon involve a combination of sensory imput, visual, kinesthetic, as well as tactile. At a given moment he may be giving himself verbal directions or reacting to the verbal instructions from an external source. And although there are limits as to the amount of information from several sources to which an individual can attend, it is apparent that gross bodily movements represent an important learning modality which has not been fully exploited by educators.

Within the past year we have designed playgrounds which encourage teachers of retarded and immature children to utilize bodily movements as learning experiences. These playground modifications were prompted by several studies from our laboratory, which demonstrated that the acquisition of gross movement patterns at times influenced the acquisition of small movement patterns and that characteristics of serial memory ability measured in verbal tasks were parallel to the same ability evidenced when individuals attempted to integrate a series of movements (5,9).

Furthermore, the studies of E. Dean Ryan and others have indicated that there are individuals who seem to block stimuli presented to them kinesthetically and visually and prefer rather to move, creating their own input. These "reducers," it could be hypothesized, may learn best by exposure to tasks upon which their inclination to move is capitalized (31).

These playground markings have been of three kinds, intended to enhance serial memory ability, pattern recognition, and spelling and number manipulations. For example, grids six feet by six feet have been painted, containing squares one foot by one foot. Within the squares in some of these grids have been placed letters, while others contain numbers. Thus a child, by jumping or hopping from square to square, can not only improve the components of agility contained in the activity itself, but also through gross movement can improve his spelling and numerical abilities. Perhaps the active "reducer" of input stimuli alluded to in the previous paragraph can learn more effectively through this modality. Research is presently in progress which will clarify this point.

Other markings involve a series of lines, squares, and zigzags which not only present the children the opportunity to practice the perceptual-motor attributes necessary to negotiate the lines, squares, etc., but are intended to improve their ability to order a series of events correctly. The extent to which the child can accomplish remembering one, two, or more things in a series is also made quite apparent to the observing teacher. For if a child cannot remember a series of two or three movements chained together, how can he be expected to spell a three-letter word in which letters must be placed and remembered in correct order?

Pattern-recognition practice on the part of immature and atypical children has been encouraged through the use of triangles, rectangles and half-circles placed on playgrounds in addition to the traditional squares and circles usually found there. Teachers working with children on shape recognition, using tactile and visual modalities within the classroom, then take them to the playground where the children attempt to discover similar shapes, name them, play on them, in them, and around them in various ways. This type of transfer must be taught, rather than being expected to occur incidentally. In any case it appears that this is another important way in which gross motor activities can contribute to basic concepts helpful in the formation of basic perceptions underlying letter recognition, word recognition, and reading (6).

More basic than these perceptions, it is believed, are those involving the child's body, its parts, and its position in space relative to objects. A sixteen-step, body-image sequence has been designed utilizing movement as well as tactile and visual training methods. If a child is not aware of these gross and subtle things about himself and his environment, it is doubtful if he can be expected to formulate more complex judgments inherent in many classroom learning tasks (6).

PROBLEM SOLVING THROUGH MOVEMENT

Muska Mosston has recently presented a theoretical framework in which it was purposed that a child can be led in an orderly manner from situations in which he simply responds to commands, to situations in which he actively engages in problem solving and evidences the quality of his decisions through movement. Although this conceptual framework is too global for a thorough review here, it is believed a helpful one to consider when one reviews mental-motor relationships (27).

Mosston suggests that teachers be conscious of four developmental channels—the mental, physical, emotional, and social—when designing learning situations. He states that a child can become self-determining and creative if an orderly transfer of decision making is made from the instructor to the child when the latter appears ready to assume decisions about the task, evaluation, and pre-performance considerations relative to intensity, time and place in which the performance will take place.

A student of mine is preparing an investigation of the extent to which we can encourage that which is termed "response generalization" among mongoloids. It will then be seen whether this kind of child can not only invent additional ways of line jumping (engage in choice-making behavior), but can become able to invent ways of jumping into squares and gain the ability to make decisions about other tasks not related to the training task.

Gross movement affords teachers an opportunity to inspect the quality of various components of problem-solving behavior in a rather direct way. To suggest that problem solving can only be engaged in within the confines of a classroom is to ignore this important method of intellectual expression.

SUMMARY

It has been attempted to outline various ways in which intellectual and motor performance may be related within the educational setting. When possible, specific methods of exploiting movement experiences as a helpful learning modality were presented.

The findings presented in these pages must be evaluated carefully, for most of them only infer causality by indirect inference through the discovery of relationships. For example, practice in "slowed-down" motor activities may not aid in causing attention-span lengthening and the resultant intellectual improvement, even though a relationship has been demonstrated (26). Further research is necessary to elucidate whether various kinds of perceptual-motor training programs and components of these programs actually result in the improvement of other kinds of desirable behavior.

One frequently hears about the role of perceptual-motor activities in the education of young children. It is believed that the term *perceptual-motor* not only indicates a growing awareness on the part of educators and physical educators that the perceptual process, the formation of judgments, is important to the ultimate motor expression which comes out of the child, but at the same time indicates that intellectual growth on the part of the child can be encouraged by manipulating the complexity of the perceptual input in intelligent ways.

A human is a single integrated organism. For convenience, we frequently fragment his behaviors in order to study them more closely or to attempt to change them in various ways. At the same time, we should remain aware, however, of the manner in which verbal, perceptual, motor, and cognitive behaviors may be inter-related.

REFERENCES

1. Abercrombie, M.L.J.; Gardiner, P.A.; Hansen, E.; Jonckheere, J.; Lindon, R.L.; Solomon, G., and Tyson, M.C.: Visual perceptual and visuomotor impairment in physically handi-

capped children. *Percept Motor Skills* (Monogr. Supply.), 3-*V18*, 1964.

2. Courts, F.A.: Relations between muscular tension and performance. *Psychol Bull, 39:347*, 1942.

3. Cratty, Bryant J.: Recency vs. primacy in a complex gross motor task. *Res Quart, 34:3*, 1963.

4. Cratty, Bryant J.: The perceptual-motor attributes of mentally retarded children and youth (Monogr.). Mental Retardation Services Board of Los Angeles County, August 1966.

5. Cratty, Bryant J.: The influence of small-pattern practice upon large-pattern learning. *Res Quart, 33:523*, 1962.

6. Cratty, Bryant J.: *Developmental Sequences of Perceptual-Motor Tasks.* Baldwin, New York, Educational Activities, Inc. 1967.

7. Cratty, Bryant J.: Motor learning. In *The Science and Medicine of Exercise and Sport.* Warren Johnson (Ed.), New York, Macmillan, 1968.

8. Cratty, Bryant J.: A three-level theory of perceptual-motor behavior. *Quest, VI: 3*, 1966.

9. Cratty, Bryant J.: Comparison of verbal-motor performance and learning in serial memory tasks. *Res Quart, 34:431*, 1964.

10. Dayton, Glenn O., Jr.; Jones, Margaret H.; Steele, Barry, and Rose, Marvin: Developmental study of coordinated eye movements in the human infant. *Arch Ophthal (Chicago)*, 71:870.

11. Delacato, Carl H.: *The Diagnosis and Treatment of Speech and Reading Problems.* Springfield, Thomas, 1963.

12. Dennis, Wayne: Infant development under conditions of restricted practice and of minimum social stimulation. *Genet Psychol Monogr, 23:143*, 1941.

13. Duffy, E.: *Activation and Behavior.* New York, Wiley, 1962.

14. Freeman, G.L.: The optimal muscular tensions for various performances. *Amer J Psychol, 51:* 146, 1938.

15. Goldfarb, W.: The effects of early institutional care on adolescent personality. *J Exp Educ, 12:106*, 1943.

16. Gray, Philip H.: Theory and evidence of imprinting in human infants. *J Psychol, 46:155*, 1958.

17. Gutin, Bernard: Effect of a short treadmill run to exhaustion on performance of long addition.

18. Haith, Marshall M.: The response of the human newborn to visual movement. *J Exp Child Psychol, 3:235*, 1966.

19. Held, Richard: Plasticity in sensory-motor systems, *Sci Amer, 213(5):8*, 1965.

20. Hess, Eckhart H: Two conditions limiting critical age for imprinting. *J Comp Physiol Psychol, 52:515*, 1959.

21. Howe, C.: A comparison of motor skills of mentally retarded and normal children. *Exceptional Child, 175:959*, 1961.

22. Humphrey, James H.: How children learn to read through physical education. *Child Learning Through Elementary School Physical Education.* Dubuque, Iowa, Brown, 1966.
23. Kephart, Newell C.: *The Slower Learner in the Classroom.* Columbus, Ohio, C.E. Merrill,
24. Kilpatrick, F. P.: Two processes in perceptual learning. *J Exp Psychol, 36:*187, 1946.
25. Keogh, Barbara K., and Jack F.: Pattern copying and pattern walking performance of normal and educationally subnormal boys. Unpublished study, UCLA, 1967.
26. Maccoby, Eleanor E.; Dowley, Edith M, and Hagen, John W.: Activity level and intellectual functioning in normal pre-school children. *Child Develop, 36:*761, 1965.
27. Mosston, Muska: *Teaching Physical Education from Command to Discovery.* Columbus, C. E. Merrill, 1966.
28. Oliver, James: The effects of physical conditioning exercises and activities on the mental characteristics of educationally subnormal boys. *Brit J Psychol,* 155, June 1958.
29. Piaget, Jean: *The Construction of Reality in the Child.* New York, Basic Books, 1954.
30. Rousseau, J.J.: *Emile on Education,* Trans. by B. Foxley. London, Dent, 1911.
31. Ryan, Dean E.: Kinesthetic figural aftereffects and athletic performance. Speech presented to National Convention of American Assn. of Health, Recreation and Phys. Ed., Chicago, 1966.
32. Shaw, W.A.: Facilitating effects of induced tension upon the perception span for digits. *Exp Psychol, 51:*113, 1956.
33. Stauffacher, J.C.: The effect of induced muscular tension upon various phases of the learning process. *Exp Psychol, 51:*113, 1956.

Chapter 2

A THREE-LEVEL THEORY OF
PERCEPTUAL-MOTOR BEHAVIOR

T HE STUDENT of human behavior arrives at valid inferences by observing people and through the careful collection and analysis of meaningful data. When conflicts arise between behavior as observed and behavior as measured, they may be resolved either by a reexamination of the rationale upon which investigations have been based, by a reassessment of evaluative procedures, and/or through the development of theoretical models which attempt to synthesize the data of observations and of measurement.

In the study of perceptual-motor behaviors, a primary conflict arises between (a) the common observation that some individuals seem to evidence proficiency in a number of skills and (b) the frequent experimental finding that "skill is specific." Proponents of the generality of perceptual-motor skill continue to utilize such terms as coordination, agility, and balance as though they were unitary factors applicable to a variety of situations. These individuals persist in the invention of various movement exercises which are purported to transfer to a variety of specific situations.

The strict experimentalist, on the other hand, seems to suggest that the specificity of perceptual-motor attributes is so marked that the only way in which an athletic team may defeat another is to actually confront them on a given day and at a given place. Researchers suggest that no amount of preparation can really duplicate

Reprinted from *Quest*, VI:3, May 1966.

the exact circumstances that will be encountered on the day of a confrontation between two teams. Furthermore, it is usually stated that transfer between skills occurs with such infrequency that practicing for transfer would seem a waste of time.

The argument concerning the specificity or generality of human attributes has had a relatively long history in the experimental literature. Spearman, in 1904, was one of the early advocates of the generality of human intelligence (24). His initial study utilized the then new tool of factor analysis. In subsequent years Guilford, Thurstone, and others interested in human cognition have suggested that intellectual behavior is highly specific, and may be fractionalized into several components (15, 27).

Experimentalists interested in perceptual-motor functioning have added further evidence to both sides of the argument concerning the specificity versus generality of human skill. Henry and his students, for example, argue for the specificity of movement speed, strength, and reaction time (17). They have found that even endurance is specific to the movement; and therefore, to suggest that a general state of cardiovascular readiness to perform is inaccurate. Rather, they suggest that one must consider endurance at doing *what* to be scientifically accurate (1). Edwin Fleishman and his colleagues have factored manual ability into five components, strength has been divided into four parts, while balance has been fractured into four balances (11).

Is there then a hypothetical construct, a meaningful and scientifically accurate model, which is compatible both with the experimental findings and common observations of human skill? Is there a lucid explanation which accurately portrays the situation as it actually is with regard to the performance and learning of perceptual-motor tasks? Several have constructed such a model to explain intellectual performance. Spearman, for example, speaks both of a "g" (general) and an "s" factor in intelligence (25). Thurstone and Kelley have also maintained that mental operations are governed by both a common primary factor as well as by specific factors (29,19). Burt, Eysenck, and Vernon share the opinion that intellectual attainment is molded by a general or universal factor at the top of a hierarchy of second-level group factors (3,10,30). Vernon postulates that second-order visual educational factors and practical-mechanical factors underlie human thinking. At the base of Vernon's pyramidal construct are placed specific, unique factors influencing a trait or test (30). Burt further divides these kinds of specific factors into "accidental factors" (those largely due to chance), and factors specific to the situation (3).

In a previous effort to resolve this general problem as related to perceptual-motor functioning, this writer proposed a theory which suggested that constructs at two levels mold performance: those specific to the task, and general ones such as the ability to analyze an activity, freedom from excess tension, and the like (6). The statement which follows represents a refinement of this model. A framework is proposed which is composed of factors at three levels. It is believed that this refined statement does not conflict with the available experimental evidence, but on the contrary is rather a comprehensive consideration of the results from a variety of types of studies; investigations which support the supposition that general kinds of behavioral tendencies support and mold perceptual-motor performance and learning, and research which indicates that skilled output is highly specific.

This theory assumes that factors at three levels influence final performance and learning output. At the base level (we are inverting Vernon's Pyramid) are *general behavioral supports,* including aspiration level, arousal, ability to analyze a task, and perhaps various perceptual abilities. Attributes at this level, it is believed, can be demonstrated to influence a variety of kinds of human behavior, including verbalization, cognition, tasks which might be classified as intellectual as well as perceptual-motor abilities. These qualities at the base of our pyramid are relatively fixed but in turn are influenced and modified by an individual's self-assessments of performance attained.

At the second level are various perceptual-motor factors spawned by the factorial studies. *Ability traits* such as static strength, extent flexibility, and the like are placed here. These intermediate traits are influential of perceptual-motor performance and are usually not demonstrated as supportive of cognition or verbal behavior.

At the apex of the triangle are placed *factors specific to the task and situation.* Such factors as the unique energy demands of the task, the immediate values impinging upon the motivational state of the performer, the perceptual components specific to the task, the unique kinds of past experiences in the task, the practice conditions, the social characteristics of the situation in which the task is performed, as well as the task's specific movement patterns (i.e. *force* requirements and *velocities*) may be found here.

This three-level theory may thus be diagrammed as follows on page 27.

Experimental evidence supporting the existence and importance of general factors named may be found at several sources. The work of Frank, for example, supports the importance of a general level of aspiration operative to support performance (14). More recent evidence collected as the University of California at Davis, by Ryan also supports the supposition that an individual's feelings about his performance potential and strivings may influence performance and learning in a diversity of tasks (23). These latter investigations found that overachievers possessing only moderate intellectual endowments who were securing high grades within a university setting also reached superior levels of achievement on a text of perceptual-motor ability.

The recent review of the literature on arousal and activation by Duffy supports the contention that individuals not only are activated to meet specific demands placed upon them in a given situation, but also habitually function at a predictable level of arousal throughout the day (9). Duffy cites innumerable investigations which support the contention that a general level of arousal unique to each individual influences the manner in which a variety of perceptual-motor activities are performed. Additional evidence from Magoun and his co-workers interested in the reticular activating system supports the importance of general activation level in the formation of behavior(21).

Studies by this writer and his students also support the inference that a general spatial factor, independent of the musculature involved in a task, influences the ability to perform skills (5,7,8). These studies indicate that musculature and spatial dimensions of the task are controlled by separate neural mechanisms and that a general spatial factor may be operative in a variety of perceptual-motor activities involving accurate movement.

The factorial work of Fleishman and his co-workers indicates that the ability to analyze the mechanics and spatial dimensions of tasks influences learning and performance, particularly during the initial stages of skill acquisition (12). An investigation by Kreiger (20) indicates that figure-ground perception may be influential of the ability to intercept balls in a variety of situations; while the investigation by Benson indicates that accurate perception of residual muscular tension contributes to relaxed and efficient performance in swimming (2).

Several investigations also indicate that with sustained practice in groups of skills, higher intercorrelations will result. These kinds of findings indicate that many of the investigations which purport to investigate transfer specifics and intercorrelations of performance levels may produce confounding results, because they may be actually sampling performances on several different points on curves based upon learning schedules which were initiated long before the adult subjects found themselves in the experimental situation. Hebb, for example, suggests that transfer of skill in adult subjects has already occurred prior to the experimental examination of transfer (16).

There is an indication that skill specificity may

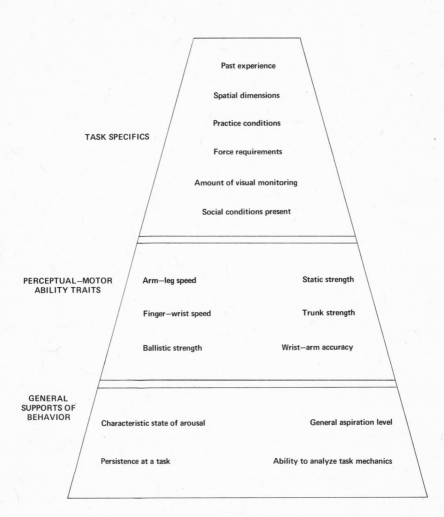

hinge upon the use of vision when performing motor acts. Transfer seems more likely in tasks when vision is eliminated than when vision accompanies complex co-ordinations. The neurological evidence relating to the vast amount of the brain devoted to visual functioning, as well as the complexity of the visual cortex, supports the contention that visual-motor performance may be highly specific, while movements performed in the absence of vision may be more highly related. Cells in the fovea of the eye are represented in the brain at a 1:1 ratio, while muscle receptors are probably afforded no such liberal representation in the cortex.

Evidence that skilled output is also governed by factors specific to the task and to the situation is also abundant. Strong's investigation, for example, clearly points to the influence of specific motivating conditions related to the social context upon measures of fitness (26). The innumerable studies by Henry and his students also attesting to the specificity of motor output have been mentioned (17,18). Namikas and others have also found that extreme specificity is evidenced when the performances of highly similar tasks are contrasted (22). Some recent factor analyses may be criticized insofar as the initial matrices obtained, containing low correlations, were further subjected to factor analyses in an attempt to isolate factors which in truth may not have been present. The recent investigation by Alderman points to the high specificity of apparently similar endurance tasks (1).

Declarations, therefore, that perceptual-motor skill is either specific or general become indefensible. The shape of the typical motor learning curve attests to the influence of past experience during the "discovery phase" of learning. The learner, during the initial stages of learning in action seems to organize the required response pattern by reference to similar activities within his repertoire of past experience.

On the other hand, for the coach or physical education teacher to ignore the specifics of skill acquisition is also fraught with peril. Particular problems will be generally encountered when attempting to elicit a new response pattern with a situation containing stimuli similar to those in a previous situation.

The effective teacher should thus be sensitive to these three levels of influence upon perceptual-motor performance, and particular attention should be directed toward their mutual influence. The lower levels constitute the basic orientation and alertness of the performer, but in turn are influenced by his constant assessment of the performance output at the apex of the construct. Ability traits within the middle of the model are influential not only of the particular task under consideration, but to varying degrees of other and similar perceptual-motor activities. Ability traits in turn are changed if the individual continues to practice activities which enhance these attributes or begins to avoid activities which result in a diminution of certain movement capacities.

Developmentally the varying importance of the three levels of factors probably change. For example, during infancy and early childhood the influence of ability traits and general supports from the lower two levels are perhaps more influential on performance. During later childhood, adolescence and adulthood, more importance might be attached to the specific influences at the apex of the pyramid.

The previous statements may seem to assume that the writer considers the intellectual and perceptual-motor functioning of man as separate behaviors. Essentially, it is believed that while human behavior may not be fragmented when subjected to philosophical speculations, scientific inquiry demands that at times we consider behavior in the plural. There seems to be kinds of behavior which, when observed, would likely be classified as either verbal, perceptual, motor, cognitive, etc.

The conceptual framework presented, it is believed, represents only transitory truth. However, at the same time it would seem to begin to explain factors which cause human movement as they really exist. Consideration of these levels of factors, it is believed, may aid in the teaching-learning process, particularly as the instructor gains first an awareness of their relative influence upon the task at hand and then becomes able to discriminate between those which are modifiable in a short period of time versus factors which are relatively fixed.

Several of the previous assumptions need further verification in the form of scholarly research. For example, the generality versus specificity of human skill as a function of the amount of visual monitoring necessary is in need of further clarification. Particular emphasis should be placed upon the extent to which various perceptual qualities underlie several kinds of perceptual-motor skills. Such factors as perceptual anticipation, figure-ground perception, and similar attributes need further clarification with particular emphasis placed upon determining whether they contribute to a group of skills or only to specific skills. To state that "skill is specific" is not very helpful, as most of the teaching-learning process cannot duplicate the multitude of conditions which later might be encountered by the learner. Thus, it is believed that the search for basic, general factors which mold a number of kinds of perceptual motor performances should be continued with vigor. Failure to consider the basic perceptual-motor capacities and the reasons for superior and inferior functioning in movement tasks constitutes a serious omission from a scholarly discourse on the total human personality.

REFERENCES

1. Alderman, Richard B.: Specificity of individual differences in arm movement fatigue within two levels of work load. *Res Quart, 36:227, 1965.*
2. Benson, David: Effects of concomitant learning in relaxation and swimming improvement (unpublished study). University of California, Los Angeles, 1958.
3. Burt, C.: *The Factors of the Mind.* London, U. of London, 1956.
4. Buxton, E.E., and Humphreys, L.G.: The effect of practice upon intercorrelations of motor skills. *Science, 81:441, 1935.*
5. Cohen, Paul: Performance times in large maze tasks (Master's Thesis). University of California, Los Angeles, 1963.

6. Cratty, Bryant J.: *Movement Behavior and Motor Learning*. Philadelphia, Lea and F., 1967.

7. Cratty, Bryant J.: The influence of small-pattern practice upon large pattern learning. *Res Quart*, 33:523, 1962.

8. Cratty, Bryant J.: A comparison of the learning of a fine motor skill to learning a similar gross motor task, based upon kinesthetic cues. *Res Quart*, 33:212, 1962.

9. Duffy, Elizabeth: *Activation and Behavior*. New York, Wiley, 1962.

10. Eysenck, H.J.: *The Structure of Human Personality*. London, Methune, 1953.

11. Fleishman, Edwin A., and Ellison, Gaylor D.: A factor analysis of fine manipulative tests. *J Appl Psychol*, 46:96, 1962.

12. Fleishman, Edwin A., and Hempel, Walter E., Jr.: Changes in factor structure of a complex psychomotor test as a function of practice. *Psychometrika*, 19:239, 1954.

13. Fleishman, E.A., and Hempel, W.E., Jr.: The relation between abilities and improvement with practice in visual discrimination reaction task. *J Exp Psychol*, 49:301, 1955.

14. Frank, J.D.: Recent studies of the level of aspiration. *Psychol Bull*, 38:218, 1941.

15. Guilford, J.P.: The structure of intellect. *Psychol Bull*, 53:267, 1956.

16. Hebb, D.O.: *The Organization of Behavior*. New York, Wiley, 1949.

17. Henry, Franklin: Increased response latency for complicated movements and "memory drum" theory of neuromotor reaction. *Res Quart*, 31:488, 1960.

18. Henry, Franklin, and Whitely, J.D.: Relationships between individual differences in strength, speed, and mass in an arm movement. *Res Quart*, 31:24, 1960.

19. Kelley, T.L.: *Crossroads in the Mind of Man*. Stanford, Stanford, 1928.

20. Kreiger, Jane C.: The influence of figure-ground perception on spatial Adjustment in Tennis (M.A. Thesis). University of California, Los Angeles, 1962.

21. Magoun, H.W.: *The Waking Brain*. Springfield, Thomas, 1958.

22. Namikas, Gediminas, and Archer, E. James: Motor skill transfer as a function of inter-task interval and pre-transfer task difficulty. *J Exp Psychol*, 59:109, 1960.

23. Ryan, Dean E.: Relative academic achievement and stabilometer performance. *Res Quart*, 34:185, 1963.

24. Spearman, C.: General intelligence objectivity measured and determined. *Amer J Psychol*, 15:201, 1904.

25. Spearman, C.: *The Abilities of Man: Their Nature and Measurement*. London, Macmillan, 1927.

26. Strong, Clinton H.: Motivation related to performance of

physical fitness test. *Res Quart, 34:*497, 1963.
27. Thurstone, L.L.: The vectors of the mind. *Psychol Rev, 41:*1, 1934.
28. Thurstone, L.L.: *Primary Mental Abilities.* Chicago, U. of Chicago, 1938.
29. Thurstone, L.L.: *Some Primary Abilities in Visual Thinking.* Chicago, U. of Chicago, Psychometric Laboratory Report, 1950.
30. Vernon, P.E.: *The Structure of Human Abilities.* London, Methune, 1953.

Chapter 3

SOME SOCIAL DIMENSIONS OF PHYSICAL ACTIVITY: RECENT TRENDS IN THE LITERATURE

WHILE SURVEYING the literature in preparation for the writing of a text on motor learning, I was struck by the overriding importance of various aspects of the social clime upon motor performance and learning. For example, psychologists differentiate between "harm" anxiety and "failure" anxiety, suggesting that the latter reflects social pressure upon performance. Studies by MacArthur and others have suggested that a general quality of persistence under social stimulation is present in a variety of mental and motor tasks. Theories of perception have arisen which indicate the importance of the sociocultural context upon perception. Studies of aspiration level also indicate that success or failure in a task is invariable measured against some norms we set for ourselves based upon our perceptions of respectable scores achievable by one of our experience and sex.

Findings of this type prompted me three years ago to embark upon another text describing the social dimensions of physical activity in more exact detail. I believe a second thing that influenced me toward this second undertaking was the barrage of propaganda to which many of us are subjected while undergraduates relative to the influence of participation in physical endeavors to social adroitness, leadership capabilities, personal adjustment and similar personality traits. Thus I attempted during the past three years to confirm or reject

A Speech at San Fernando Valley State College, Northridge, California, May 3, 1966.

some of the folklore that has been propagated relative to sociality-performance relationships.

The findings I will present to you today are selective rather than exhaustive. Essentially, they were things which were new and interesting to me; facts which I believe may prove useful when working with groups of people engaged in vigorous activity. Many of these findings have arisen from studies whose experimental protocols are somewhat superficial. Similar to studies of motor learning found in the psychological journals, many of these investigations surveyed in social psychology utilized a motor skill only to obtain an exact performance measure rather than because of an interest in the motor act itself on the part of the experimenter.

Essentially, I was interested in exploring variables which the sociologists term "human interactions;" small group relationships, leadership, group cohesion, personal goal-setting, maturation as influential of sociality in performance situations, and the effects of various subcultures (family, peer group, etc.) upon physical capacity and participation. These are variables which have not been surveyed in any organized way by physical education texts; and while there is a growing trend to examine various psychological variables and their relationship to performance output and the influence of the broad, general cultural context upon the selection of activities available to people, the important and numerous variables between the individual and the cultural context have been accorded relatively little attention.

GENDER IDENTIFICATION IN CHILDREN

I have conducted a clinical program for the improvement of children with mild perceptual-motor problems during the past several years. On several occasions I have been confronted with boys whose movement characteristics suggest that they have problems identifying with a member of their own sex. They failed to express agression appropriately, they moved and exhibited facial expressions similar to those expected in girls, and in other ways were having problems with peer relationships. I was confronted with this same kind of problem while giving a symposium at the Texas Institute of Child Psychiatry in Houston last December. A boy was brought into the room who exhibited marked feminine characteristics and various specialists evaluated his behavior.

With the help of several experts at UCLA's Neuro Psychiatric Institute and Department of Psychology, I began to review literature relevant to this problem and found the following to be current consensus: (a) This behavior is quite complex and evidenced at an extremely early age; (b) Far less experimental and societal attention is paid to the masculine girl, than to the feminine boy; (c) This atypical behavior is evidenced more frequently in homes where the father is ineffectual or absent and the mother is dominant, and where there is a predominance of siblings of the opposite sex; (d) this behavior can be evaluated by two means: the Games Test, and the IT test; (e) It has been hypothesized that gender preference is the result of early human imprinting, similar to imprinting seen in animals.

The most striking finding that I was confronted with was a statement by an expert on male homosexuality who informed that over 70 per cent of the males whom she interviewed said that their confrontation with physical activities appropriate to males was a traumatic experience in their lives; that they did not do well at them, actively sought help which was not available, and at this time retreated further from things masculine.

And while I do not intend to pass moral judgement on adult deviant behavior, it is apparent that children behaving inappropriately as compared to one of their biological sex suffer social rejection and severe trauma. Thus, it seems to me that it is indicated that male and female physical educators could be sensitive to this problem in children and provide appropriate models of appearance and behavior which such children can emulate, but more than that, should seek out such children and work with them in constructive ways which might help them to acquire movement patterns appropriate to one of their sex.

GROUP NEEDS VERSUS GROUP PERFORMANCE

A second type of problem began to interest me follow-ing a study we conducted at UCLA in 1961. It became apparent upon surveying the research in group inter-action that individuals brought two kinds of basic needs to a group: (a) the need for affiliation, for fellowship, for belonging, and (b) the need for achievement, for good performance, for success. Many times these needs were relatively balanced, i.e. the person wanted both, and one enhanced the other. However, there were indications that there is an optimum level of group cohesion pro-ductive of maximum group output.

For example, in the study cited above, groups who were highly cohesive (i.e. members of fraternity pledge classes), and groups who were not (they did not know each other prior to participation in the experiment) were brought together and permitted to interact between trials in a large maze task. Contrary to our hypothesis, it was found that the groups meeting there specifically to per-form the task were far more successful than the groups who had been previously aligned socially. Interactions between the fraternity groups frequently digressed to discussions of the next weekend's social activities rather than being related to the task at hand. Social "noise" seemed to interfere with good group performance.

Studies carried out in the middle 1950's in Illinois, surveying the cohesiveness of high school basketball teams, further elucidate this principle. Teams whose win-loss records were average scored higher on a scale measuring group cohesion than did teams whose win-loss records were decidedly superior. Particularly it was noted that superior teams often evidenced hostility on the part of superior performers toward the less skilled. Other investigations indicate that work-partner choice is related to whether the chooser has high need for affiliation or achievement; in the former instance a friend is invariably chosen, while in the latter case a good performer is selected as a teammate. A recent study of leaders on high school basketball teams in

Idaho and Utah indicated that frequently the team leader was not the best liked.

While it is apparent that a moderate amount of group cohesion is necessary in order not to dissipate leadership energy and to carry out the task at hand, the current literature suggests that much of the group member's energies must be directed toward achievement, rather than toward being affiliated for the warm feelings it brings. While the coach should certainly not encourage strained relationships among team members, he should probably not become overly concerned when he sees and hears evidence of group tensions, particularly if that evidence indicates that the boys care more about winning than about each other.

PARENTAL TRAINING FOR ACHIEVEMENT

A shift in trend in child-rearing literature which has become apparent during the past several years concerns a redirection of emphasis from producing the adjusted child to the stimulation of achievement in children. A study by Rosen and D'Andrade illustrates the differences in child-parent interactions which might be expected between children whose achievement needs are marked versus the apathetic child. After identifying twenty boys with high versus twenty with low achievement needs (using a projective test), permission was gained to enter their homes and with the cooperation and participation of their parents, administer four tests, three of which were motor, or at least perceptual-motor in character. The parents were encouraged to participate to the fullest, talking to the boys (9,10,11 years), and otherwise getting goals in some instances (i.e. deciding how far from a quoit stick to place the child), and otherwise interacting with the child. Both experimenters recorded comments from the parents and children.

In general it was found that marked differences existed between the parent-child behaviors in the homes of the high versus low achievers. High achievers' parents seemed to engage in self-reliance training, setting high goals, encouraging generally rather than offering specific information, and otherwise stimulating the child to succeed. The low achievers were given goals by the parents which permitted high scores rather than offering a challenge, were given specific information on how to perform, etc. The children in the former case frequently refused help, while the low achievers sought help. The scores of the high achievers were higher, while those of the low achievers were inferior.

The fathers were seen to be crucial in the relationship. Their comments proved more crushing or supportive than did the comments extended by the mothers to their performing sons. Likewise the high achievers always had at least one parent who engaged in self-reliance training, while the lower achievers had neither parent sensitively "pulling them from ahead."

Several questions arise from the consideration of such findings: How specific is achievement training by parents? Does it extend into physical and intellectual endeavors or is it more specifically directed? What is the influence of maternal behavior on the performance of girls in the family? Investigations of this nature, however, do indicate that much of a child's values for success are not related to what happens to him at school but are the result of a subtle and constant kind of parental behavior to which he has been subjected rather early in life.

CONCLUSIONS

The literature in social psychology questions many of the assumptions jumping out at us from the typical method books in physical education during the past several decades. For example, it is apparent that friendships are formed primarily on the basis of similarity in interests and with people who are in constant physical proximity to one another. The assumption that close interaction must be in physical skills to produce friendships is unfounded; studies carried out in offices and in housing developments attest to the importance of really analyzing the variables one at a time before assigning such an important role to the physical components of such interaction.

The role of athletic participation in the formation of leadership qualities has been assumed by physical educators as an important one for many years. And yet recent research emanating from West Point indicated that when boys who were termed athletes and non-athletes at entrance were confronted with compulsory participation in competitive athletics during a four-year period, their personality complex did not change. The athletes were as significantly different from the non-athletes at the end of four years as they were at the beginning, based upon the measurement of selected personality traits.

But a thorough study of this literature has made me even more aware of the overriding importance of the social context upon performance; we may never divorce ourselves from it even when we are placed alone in a room under the jurisdiction of some experimenter, for will he not know our score? And what will he do with it? The recent investigation by Strong suggests that physical fitness scores are more a function of the social situation in which they are administered and the social motivators that are applied than being dependent upon strength and endurance qualities of the testees.

It is believed important for a physical educator and coach to become aware of these subtle social influencers of performance, and when possible to manipulate the social context in ways helpful not only to performance improvement, but to affect improvement in the personality of those participating. It is important to know what we can change socially (i.e. team membership, leadership) and what is little modified by our efforts (i.e. family influences) and then to act accordingly. Because people will change each other and will change when performing in groups, it is part of our job to see that the direction of this change will be in ways which are helpful to the personality of the participant in our charge.

Chapter 4

THE COMPLEXITY OF PEOPLE

During the past year I have been engaged one day a week as a consultant for the special education branch of the Los Angeles City Schools. It has been my job to travel from school to school and work with retardates and neurologically handicapped children and at the same time demonstrate sequences of various kinds of perceptual-motor tasks helpful to the total educational effort made in their behalf. During this period of time I have observed children who exhibit a minimum of complexity of behavior. They deal only with the here and now; they do not seem to be able to manipulate abstractions, nor do they seem to be able to call upon past experiences to solve immediate problems with which they are faced. Examination of various intellectual and motor ability scores gleaned from such a population confirms the fact that truly their abilities are not highly complex or diversified. Typically moderate to high intercorrelations are obtained when their scores on various intellectual and motor tasks are compared (4).

At the same time in normal children we see early behavior which is primarily perceptual-motor in nature, but which quickly tends to diversify as late infancy and early childhood is reached. Normal children frequently engage in immobile thought, and when moving in complex ways think about their movements. Occupational therapists term this thinking about movement *motor planning*, psychologists talk about the adoption of helpful

Speech to the State Convention of the California Association for Health, Physical Education, and Recreation, held in Los Angeles, March 20, 1967.

work methods, while a recent writer in the field of physical education has devised what he has termed a *spectrum of styles* to enhance thinking through movement experiences (8).

I believe a basic question which people working with children and adolescents must ask themselves is to what extent will they allocate various decisions about the activity to the students. How much will they permit the student to think about what he is about to do, and to evaluate the success of his efforts?

To many, an overriding objective of physical education is the production of physical fitness. The impetus of the Fitness Councils first established by President Eisenhower and given further attention by Presidents Kennedy and Johnson had as its sole objective the establishment of programs of vigorous activities intended to heighten cardiorespiratory endurance and muscular strength. Films have been produced indicating how obstacle courses can provide motivating kinds of physical experiences which will enhance these attributes; at the same time various state committees and councils have been established to implement programs whose outlines have been suggested by the President's Council. Our own State of California, not to be left behind, has been active in this effort. The production of various tests and norms as well as of program suggestions have been the outcome.

As is the case when an authority suggests that some kind of operational or philosophical change be made in program emphasis, administrators of educational programs can take several courses of action: They can ignore the suggestion; they can incorporate the ideas into their present programs; or they can overreact, devoting their entire effort toward some kind of new emphasis.

If one surveys the physical education program of the State of California, he will see a broad range of behaviors. Some are conducting a "squat and sit program" in which the instructors seem to be conducting some kind of group therapy shrouded in a protective mantle of neo-Deweyism. Others are engaged in a form of stimulus-response conditioning which would well be emulated by the animal trainers at Jungleland. On the broad mid-ground are the majority who utilize physical activities in a variety of ways to induce better physical conditions, to teach socially accepted skills, and to encourage the children to structure and to think about their actions.

It is believed that operating at either extreme of this continuum of behavior neglects the developmental phases for which we can be responsible. It is believed that an overemphasis upon either a program which stresses solely the physical development of its participants, or one which becomes preoccupied with the "why's" of everything to the exclusion of .vigorous action are equally shallow. Some of the physical fitness programs currently operative in the state produce truly astounding results. Adolescents participate in exercise programs for the privilege of wearing trunks of various colors and for receiving emblems designating their state of physical competency. It is believed, however, that educators must not simply "motivate" children to do their bidding, but must first examine philosophically just what will be important kinds of activities in which to participate not only during adolescence but in early and late adulthood.

Educators, from Rousseau through Maria Montessori to Skinner and his learning-teaching machines, have learned that they can "trick," "reinforce," or otherwise elicit various kinds of performance in children with the proper kinds of immediate rewards system. I believe, however, that educators must utilize their mature judgment to consider the long-term and well as the short-term rewards for participation in various kinds of physical activities on the part of adolescents and young adults.

Children are motivated by conditions external to the task, by social stimulation, and by various obvious rewards in the form of emblems, money and the like (2). As children mature, however, they are less susceptible to influence by various external rewards and are more likely to be motivated by their interest in the task, its novelty and complexity (6,7,9). To treat adolescents like animals, presenting only strenuous exercise programs to them during secondary school days, ignores the shift in values that are certain to occur as they mature. Colored emblems on trunks have negligible reinforcing qualities as the boy enters college and wishes to engage a young girl in a tennis game. His skill at the game is what draws him into participation, as well as perhaps the smile of the coed.

A program of activities in high school emphasizing only the physical can perhaps be attributed not only to the national and state emphasis on fitness, but perhaps also on the pronouncements emitting from some philosophers in the field. Some physical educators may retreat to the security of what they know they can do, and to activities which they know will produce obvious changes when their ears are assaulted by such phrases as "We should be interested in man in his total energy surroundings!" or perhaps "The interactions of man and his environment are important" or "Man and his earth-world should be the emphasis." These pronouncements would traumatize anyone into inaction. Such statements are relatively meaningless to the teacher on the field, as they are to many of us in the universities and colleges throughout the state. They denote nothing in the way of new practices, nor do they spur scholarly research. These phrases seem to be a method of meeting one's needs to sound important and end up by not only saying nothing, but by driving communication wedges between university and secondary school personnel. Such overcompensatory phrases seem to denote feelings of academic marginality.

But whatever the causes of the recent physical education programs, governmental edict, retreat from pedagogical redundancy, or simply the manifestation of the teacher's needs for authoritarian behavior, it is believed they are basically unsound for two primary reasons:

1. Adolescents' goals shift constantly; they participate in physical activities for entirely different reasons as young adults than they did as early and late adolescents.

2. Man is a complex, thinking animal, not simply an energy machine which reacts to specific stimuli. If decisions can be transferred from the teacher to the participants in physical education classes, more meaningful as well as more vigorous activity will usually result. Mosston has recently presented practical methods whereby this orderly transfer of decision making is possible in physical education settings. Adolescents are complex. To work with them we must accommodate to more facets of their behavior than simply the ability to exert muscular force for varying periods of time. The answer to complexity of human functioning is educational programs which provide experiences accommodating to more than one facet of adolescent behavior. The answer to complexity is not a retreat to simplicity.

REFERENCES

1. Cratty, Bryant J.: A three level theory of perceptual-motor behavior. *Quest, VI: 3,* May 1966.
2. Cratty, Bryant J.: Social motives. *In Movement Behavior and Motor Learning,* 2nd ed. Philadelphia, Lea and F., 1964.
3. Cratty, Bryant J.: The Perceptual-motor attributes of mentally retarded children and youth (Monogr.). Mental Retardation Services Board of Los Angeles County, August 1966.
4. Cratty, Bryant J.: *Social Dimensions of Physical Activity.* Englewood Cliffs, Prentice-Hall, 1967.
5. Harris, Laurren: The effects of relative novelty on children's choice behavior. *J Exp Child Psychol,* 2:297,
6. Maccoby, Eleanor E.: Dowley, Edith M., and John W. Hagen: Activity level and intellectual functioning in normal preschool children. *Child Develop,* 36:761, 1965.
7. Mendel, Giseld: Children's preferences for differing degrees of novelty. *Child Develop,* 36:452, 1966.
8. Mosston, Muska: *Teaching Physical Education,* Columbus, Ohio, C. E. Merrill, 1966.
9. Smock, Charles D., and Holt, Bess Gene: Children's reactions to novelty: An experimental study of "curiosity motivation." *Child Develop,* 33:631, 1962.

Chapter 5

THE INDEPENDENCE AND INTERDEPENDENCE OF VISUAL PERCEPTION AND MOVEMENT IN INFANTS AND CHILDREN

A CONSIDERABLE amount of attention has been directed toward exploring the role of movement in the development of perceptual attributes in infants and children. Some workers have suggested that abilities to organize the visual world are primarily dependent upon the emergence of voluntary action patterns and that motor activity is the basis of all perceptual judgments in normal children. Further extensions of this reasoning have led some to conclude that motor learning is the basis of cognitive development.

It has been advanced by some that all visual judgments depend upon the emergence of accurate movement capacities and efficient balancing abilities, and conversely, that faulty manual-visual coordinations, defective locomotor abilities, and poor balance are disruptive of all spatial judgments.

It is believed, however, that these theories must be subjected to the sword of current experimental evidence. It is with this in mind that this review was written, as it is believed that some of the simplistic statements about perceptual-motor development put forth within the past twenty years might be seriously questioned upon consideration of current research findings.

Evidence which sheds light upon some of the complex questions inherent in the title of this paper may be found

Speech presented at the Child Achievement Center, Sherman Oaks, California, July 28, 1967.

within several research programs being conducted throughout the country. Richard Held and his colleagues at M.I.T., in a series of studies using both animal and human adults and infants as subjects, seem to demonstrate the close interaction between visual judgments and self-induced movement (movement engaged in by the individual making the judgments) (20,21,22). In a typical experiment, normal human observers were given prismatic spectacles which produced systematic distortion, i.e. points in the perceived space were displaced laterally and straight lines seemed curved. If the observer was permitted to walk actively for about an hour, these distortions disappeared. If instead they were pushed through their environment in a wheelchair. they did not adapt. Similar experiments involved the dissipation of hand-eye distortions and tasks involving more static bodily orientations. They concluded that active movement was necessary for adaptation to this kind of sensory rearrangement.

K. W. Smith at the University of Wisconsin has advanced a *neurogeometric theory* of human motion based upon investigations of the manner in which humans reintegrate vision and movement after they have been experimentally "broken down" in space and time via complex television monitor video tape arrangements (32).

Werner and Wapner and their students at Clark University have evolved a sensory-tonic theory of perception based upon a number of studies in which altered postural and visual "tonus" have been demonstrated to influence kinesthetic, tactile, and visual judgments of verticality (39,40).

.Information from other sources contributes to knowledge about the interactions of vision and movement in the developing infant. O. W. Smith at Cornell University has conducted factoral analyses of visual perception as a function of age (33). Robert Fantz has demonstrated the manner in which exposure to various patterns affect the time infants visually inspect their environment, while Haith, Dayton and others have presented evidence which supports the fact that visual activity occurs from birth and may be elicited by the movement of objects across the crib, as well as by stimuli of moderate complexity inspected during the first few hours of life (13,8,18).

A synthesis of the findings of these research programs prompts the following generalizations:

1. *Visual perception is not unitary, but is composed of several independent aptitude clusters.*

For example, Smith and his colleagues have identified six distinct traits including the ability to organize movement in space, the ability to fractionalize space, the ability to estimate distance as related to size, and the ability to see clearly (visual acuity) (33). They conclude that the ability to make spatial judgments is not a general trait. These data indicate that these independent visual-perceptual traits are relatively stable from childhood to adulthood. Coan similarly demonstrates the independence of perceptual judgments involving movement, vision, and measures involving combinations of vision and movement (4). Burg and Halbert among others also have found that perception of movement and visual acuity are not closely related (3).

2. *From the first hours of birth infants engage in a remarkable amount of visual behavior.*

Haith found that moving objects across the crib of infants twenty-four to twenty-eight hours old significantly suppressed non-nutritive sucking movements (18). Dayton and his colleagues have noted that infants evidence the ability to fixate at extremely young ages, while White and Held discovered that infants a few days old evidenced visual accommodation to targets about seven and a half inches distant (8,38).

3. *This early visual behavior is not random, but involves perceptual discrimination.*

Fantz, Hershenson, Spears, and others have found that discriminative processes are apparently involved insofar as infants show definite preferences for objects which are bright, those which evidence a moderate degree of complexity, and those which are novel (12,13,14,23,36). Familiar objects in close proximity are not afforded the same degree of attention as are novel ones. There seems to be an optimum degree of complexity of design and/or shape which elicits the greatest amount of visual attention by infants.

The tendency to ignore the familiar is especially apparent at about the second month of age. It has been suggested that this tendency is one of the critical mechanisms undergirding learning. The apparent innate tendency to seek novelty and complexity has also been confirmed in studies concerned with manual exploratory activity of children and primates (30,34).

Sokolov has proposed a cortical neuronal model to account for the tendency of an orienting reflex to be elicited by novel stimuli. A cortical cell assembly, it is suggested, preserves information about the characteristics, intensity, and order of early stimuli with which novel stimuli may be compared (35). The human tends to evidence an orienting reflex when, following such comparisons, there is a lack of concordance between the presented stimuli and those of previously acquired models due to the generation of a cortical discharge to the nonspecific core brain. Continued presentation of a stimulus, Sokolov concludes, results in feedback inhibition which blocks input to the core system.

4. Rudimentary visual-perceptual behavior in infants precedes their ability to move with accuracy and to contact directly the objects in their environment by several weeks.

For example, early attempts to "swipe" at objects, which constitutes the most rudimentary of efforts to contact the environment, are not evidenced until after the fortieth day, whereas visual behavior has been observed and measured, as was stated above, within the first twenty-four hours of birth. It has been found that exposing babies to environments which are visually stimulating will delay the onset of manual activity from one to two weeks (38). In an experiment by White and Held it was found that children who had been given twenty minutes of extra handling per day from their sixth to their thirty-sixth day tended to engage in more movements of the head and trunk (perhaps to place themselves in position to see better when in their cribs. Infants whose environments were enriched were also noted by these researchers to engage in significantly greater amounts of visual inspection of objects. However, there was a significant delay of about two weeks in the onset of hand regard. Their hands were observed initially by the children in the experimental group only when they attempted to contact objects. When the seventy-second day had been reached, this early visual enrichment had manifested itself in significantly increased visual monitoring of hand and arm movements.

Thus, it would seem that while early and enriched visual experiences will facilitate visual activity, increased opportunities to see things may delay responses involving the child's own movements. Fantz, after reviewing studies of this kind, concludes: "In development, visual perception *precedes* action, rather than the reverse as is often assumed. A primitive type of perception is present from birth" (13).

5. *Early visual-motor integrations occurring when normal children contact their environment manually and attempt to move through space via locomotor behavior probably aid them to organize certain components of near and distant space. However, this manual-locomotor activity does not seem imperative to the formation of all visual-perceptual judgments.*

For example, Abercrombie, studying children who never exhibited accurate movement capacities due to brain damage to the motor cortex, found little difference when their scores in perceptual and intellectual measures were compared to the responses of normal children on the same testing instruments (1).

Even though Richard Held and his colleagues present evidence which suggests that only *self-induced* movement will correct experimentally produced visual-motor distortions in humans and will elicit certain accurate visual discriminations in infants and animals (21,22), it has been demonstrated that if adults and children are permitted to gain a cognitive awareness of the nature of an experimentally produced illusion, visual-motor reintegrations occur independent of whether their limbs are moved passively by the experimenter or if the subjects are permitted to engage in volitional movements (24). Kilpatrick, among others, has demonstrated that humans can manipulate visual space vicariously when attempting to "see through" perceptual illusions involving room-size shape changes (28). More than sixty years ago Judd found that perceptual distortions of target location placed under water could be corrected if his subjects were given information concerning principles of refraction (25). A critique of Held's work by Howard and Templeton states that it is probable that response substitution involves activity at a higher level (i.e. cortex) within the neuraxis than the level at which practiced habits occur (24). "A person may be told," they continue, "of the extent to which an optical distortion is present and may hit the displaced visual target on their first try" (24). It thus seems probable that human infants and adults can accurately organize their world visually *while* simply observing the various moving and static phenomena surrounding them.

Despite the evidence from the laboratories of Clark University delineating the sensory-tonic theory of perception and the work of Karl Smith at Wisconsin, it would seem that at times perceptual processes operate relatively independent of motoric behavior in the developing infant and child.° For if indeed, as we have stated, perceptual processes are not unidimensional, it would seem somewhat tenuous to assume that all perception is somehow related to various qualitative and/or quantitative characteristics of voluntary movement.

What then is the momentary truth? If we cannot somehow lump perception into a neat pile undergirded by the conglomerate of all voluntary action patterns, how then

---

°The sensory-tonic theory of perception has been criticized insofar as contradictory findings purport to support the same theoretical formulations and that the theory is too broad, i.e. anything can be predicted with suitable *ad hoc* assumptions, due to the absence of specific operationally definable variables (24, p. 195). Smith's theory has been criticized in that the measurements employed seem only to point to the specificity of human skill (24, p.382) rather than to any important theoretical generalizations relative to the integrations of vision and movement.

does the developing infant learn about himself and his visual world? Do these problems defy understanding? What implications does the experimental evidence have for the education of atypical children? The answers to these questions are difficult, and it is thus not without some anxiety that we try to pose tentative answers to them here. For although all the answers are not clearly discernible due to the complexity of the human nervous system and to the various channels into which infant, child, and adult behaviors may fall, the public is being inundated with theories which offer magical movement panaceas purporting to correct the perceptual difficulties of atypical infants as well as promising marked improvement in the functioning of normal youngsters. It is therefore believed that researchers have an obligation to synthesize the available evidence which does suggest sound procedures undergirding educational processes for children with physical and/or mental handicaps as well as to outline helpful movement experiences for children evidencing relatively normal development.

The following guidelines for educators are based upon the writer's interpretation of the literature and are not considered absolutes. Their validity may only be ascertained by further study concerning the interactions of visual perception, movement experiences, and educational tasks. Some of these guidelines are theoretical statements, while others suggest practical applications.

1. There are a number of separate and at times independent perceptual and motor schemata represented by aptitude clusters derived from factoral studies. °

The ability to organize movement in distant space, for example, has been found to be independent of the abil-

---

°The term *schemata* has been borrowed from Piaget and represents a group of related abilities. Some of these ability "families" have been derived primarily from factoral studies in visual perception, motor competency, and from analyses of tasks involving visual-motor integrations. It should be realized, however, that the emergence of such clusters of abilities in these investigations are a function of the type of tasks the investigator selects to compare, the age, sex, and ability level of the participating subjects, as well as the type of factor analytic methods employed.

ity to organize static near space. Similarly manual dexterity has been factored into five components; balance ability into four (33,15,16,17). Similar fractionalization has been applied to strength and to other motor attributes (17).

2. *These schemata may combine in the performance of a single complex task.*

Catching a ball, for example, probably involves the organization of movement in distant space (movement parallax), fractionalization (estimation of portions of distances), locomotor ability as the body is placed in position to intercept the missile, and hand-wrist coordination as the hands surround the ball when it arrives.

3. *Certain perceptual schemata involving visual judgments naturally pair with movements.*

The earliest of these involves what has been termed *self-observation reafference*, the visual organization of an individual's own moving body parts. Later, as the child walks he engages in what has been called *locomotor reafference*, the organization of visual stimuli as the individual walks through space (24). Accompanying the simple visual monitoring of limbs and body movements are schemata involving the perception of the shape of objects which are simultaneously visually and manually inspected. The Russians have advanced what they term a *motor copy theory* to explain the perceptions formulated in this manner. They suggest that a child "stores" copies of the shapes and objects he contacts as he matures and subsequent visual-manual explorations are compared against the stored copies in order to be identified as unique or similar to those previously encountered (35). It is obvious that at times locomotor reafference, self-observation reafference, and the manual-visual exploration of shapes and objects may occur simultaneously.

It is also apparent that another important type of visual-motor experience accompanies the locomotor and visual-manual activities described. This is engaged in by the growing infant when is too young to move himself through his environment but instead is carried by his parents. He thus may view the moving and stable spatial objects which constantly change their relationships to him and to each other from his moving space "platform." Experimentally increasing this type of visual-motor experience has been demonstrated to significantly increase the infant's later self-induced visual-motor activity both qualitatively and quantitatively (36).

4. *Perceptual schemata may be paired artifically with movements to aid in certain educational processes.*

For example, atypical children with learning difficulties may evidence problems involving the identification of simple geometric shapes or perhaps with the ordering of three or more items in a series as is necessary in spelling. Pattern recognition may be enhanced by using gross movement as a learning modality. The child may play on triangles, half-circles, squares, and simple patterns on the playground. Attempting to remember the series of steps necessary to negotiate an obstacle course may enhance seriation.

5. *Opportunities to practice "natural" pairings of perceptual and motor schemata might be increased so that children with learning difficulties may achieve competency in forming spatial judgments.*

The child who is neurologically handicapped may require additional hours of practice in integrating hand and eye movements when attempting to learn to write. Locomotor activities may need to be practiced so that the child with movement problems can engage in efficient locomotor reafferent behavior.

6. *At times educators may attempt to separate certain visual-motor pairings to enhance a child's functioning.*

For example, it is not efficient to watch one's feet when walking. Instead, the eyes should be free to explore the environment through which the child is passing. Thus balance and locomotor activities may at first be paired with vision as the child is encouraged to watch his progress on the balance beam or when walking in footprints. Later the child should be encouraged to look at spatial targets when walking and balancing. Sensitivity to the shape of objects may be enhanced by requiring that the child handle and identify objects which are placed so that they may not be seen.

7. Some perceptual-motor schemata may naturally evolve into concepts, while others may be terminal.

For example, watching the progress and characteristics of moving objects may lead toward concepts involving space, mass, velocity, and force. Learning to dress oneself may not lead toward any conceptual activity, but is simply a helpful life activity. It is a mistake, however, for educators to assume that because a child engages in efficient visual-motor interactions with his environment that he will necessarily acquire concepts arising from these activities. For example, acquiring expertise at catching balls does not necessarily lead toward an understanding of the physics of motion! It is thus important to teach specifically for transfer rather than expecting it to occur spontaneously (10). For example, it has been suggested that the child's organization of spatial dimensions, particularly the left and right of space, is related to his ability to correctly identify his left and right body parts (26). However, when this relationship was recently explored experimentally no correlation was obtained between tests of laterality and the ability to make left-right discriminations in space (2). This does not mean, however, that heightening a sense of laterality in the child cannot lead toward the correct placement of objects, words, letters in space; but such a transfer must be taught for (10)!

Accompanying the fallacy concerning transfer is the equally intellectually crippling falsehood concerning the confusion between *relationship* and *causality*. For example, because a number of symptoms may be evidenced by a child labeled neurologically handicapped, this listing gives us little information as to which of these may cause another; or which problem if corrected will ameliorate another. Although a thorough discussion of this kind of confusion requires more space and time than we have here, suffice it to say that we must constantly search for the causal effects of one behavioral facet upon another rather than inferring causality and direction of causality simply because of concurrent manifestation.

8. *Certain perceptual activities may at times be paired with movement and at other times may remain independent.*

The development of certain perceptual schemata may occur independent of any actions the infant and child may engage in. A child may simply watch moving objects, or at other times he may choose to intercept them (i.e. catch the ball). Patterns and forms may be appreciated as the child passes through the art gallery, or he may choose to participate directly in the manual inspection of forms and objects. By using clay he may form three dimensional objects himself.

SUMMARY

Research was reviewed which demonstrates the independence of various visual-perceptual aptitudes and motoric functioning. Investigations were described which explain how early visual-perceptual activity in infants begins shortly after birth and precedes accurate movements by several weeks. It was pointed out that several programs of research purporting to demonstrate the close relationship between certain components of visual perception and movement produce results which are primarily a function of specific experimental conditions rather than elucidating how children actually develop in the real world.

These findings led toward several postulates relative to perceptual-motor behavior and certain educational processes. It was suggested that there are both natural and artificial pairings of perceptual and motor aptitudes which may be engaged in in life and in the schoolroom. Certain of these artificial pairings, if carefully developed, may enhance certain components of the educational process. Atypical children may need some repetition of natural pairings of vision and movement. Some perceptual schemata, it was advanced, may evolve independent of any direct motoric involvement on the part of infants; while other visual-motor pairing may result in mutual enhancement of both visual and motor schemata. These statements, of course, suggest entire programs of research. For example, the frequently employed phrase in this paper, "at times," needs to be more exact. At just what times and in what instances are these principles operative in the life of a child? Furthermore, relationships between certain perceptual schemata and cognitive structures beg for experimental attention. At the same time, the remarkable flexibility of the human action system and sub-systems needs further elucidation. It is apparent, for example, that the blind proceed from a different base than do the sighted when formulating concepts, but are the final concepts that the sightless derive significantly different from those acquired by normal children?

Which schemata involving vision, movement, or vision and movement in concert naturally evolve into cognitive structures? What kind of transfer from percepts to concepts must be taught for? Which perceptual-motor activities terminate in no appreciable thought but are only successful when they are engaged in without thought? These and similar questions should keep researchers busy for years.

The subtle relationships between maturation, early perceptual imprinting, learning, and anxiety in the infants should be explored (6). When the interactions of these factors are more clearly outlined, an ideal learning environment for infants could result. At the present time it appears that optimum perceptual development will occur in normal infants if they are visually and tactually stimulated to a moderate degree while at the same time presented with both moving and fixed stimuli of moderate and ever-changing complexity around their cribs. At about the third and fourth month, objects to manually contact should be available to the child. Exact guidelines delineating optimum qualitative and quantitative facets of these early perceptual and perceptual-motor experiences await further research.

One of the most complex yet pressing problems is the determination of the role of ocular activity versus perceptual organization in the enhancement of the class-room skills and the acquisition of knowledge and concepts (29). Perhaps the argument as to whether reading is carried out with the eye or the brain is redundant; both are probably important. However, proponents of certain programs of sensory-motor education suggest that achieving smooth eye movements by requiring the child to watch a ball swinging on a string will enhance reading, but research indicates that in reading the eye moves in irregular stops and starts and is fixed about ninety per-cent of the time when viewing the printed page (37).

The public is becoming impatient with researchers. There is a strong feeling on the part of parents of children with learning problems that almost anything should be tried without waiting for scientific verification. At the same time there is a considerable amount of scientific evidence which clearly delineates the worth of certain educational practices involving visual-motor activity while negating other techniques. This research should continue to be synthesized and brought to the public attention in as palatable a form as possible so that the pseudo scientific outpourings from the "clinics" of certain "educationalists" does not continue to waste the time, energies, and monetary resources of atypical children and of their anxious parents.

REFERENCES

1. Abercrombie, M. L. J.; Gardiner, P. A.; Hanson, E.; Jonckheere, J.; Lindon, R. L.; Solomon, G., and Tyson, M. C.: Visual-perceptual and visuomotor impairment in physically handi-capped children. *Perceptual Motor Skills* (Monogr. Suppl.), *3-V 18*, 1964.

2. Ayres, A. Jean: Patterns of perceptual-motor dysfunction in children: A factor analytic study. *Percept Motor Skills* (Monogr. Suppl.), 1-V 20, 1965.

3. Burg, Albert, and Halbert, Slade: Dynamic visual acuity as related to age, sex, and status acuity. *J Appl Psychol*, 45:111, 1961.

4. Coan, Richard W.: Factors in movement perception. *J Consult Psychol*, 28:394, 1964.

5. Cratty, Bryant J.: *Developmental Sequences of Perceptual-*

Motor Tasks for Neurologically Handicapped and Retarded Children. Freeport, Long Island, New York, Educational Activities, 1967.

6. Cratty, Bryant J.: Human imprinting. In *New Perspectives of Man in Action*. Roscoe Brown and Bryant Cratty (Eds.). 1968 (in press).

7. Cratty, Bryant J.: *Movement Behavior and Motor Learning*, 2nd ed. Philadelphia, Leaand F., 1967.

8. Dayton, Glenn O. Jr.; Jones, Margaret H.; Steele, Barry, and Rose, Marion: Developmental study of coordinated eye movement in the human infant. *Arch Ophthal, 71:871,*

9. Dunsing, Jack, and Kephart, N.C.: Motor generalizations in space and time. In *Learning Disorders*. Bernie Straub and Jerome Hellmuth (Eds.). Seattle, Special Child Publications, Seattle Seguine School, 1966.

10. Ellis, Henry: *The Transfer of Learning*. New York, Macmillan, 1965.

11. Fantz, Robert L.: Form preferences in newly hatched chickens. *J Comp Physiol Psychol, 50:422,* 1957.

12. Fantz, Robert L.: The origin of form perception. *Sci Amer, 204:459,* 1961.

13. Fantz, Robert L.: Pattern discrimination and selective attention as determinants of perceptual development from birth. In *Perceptual Development in Children*. Aline H. Kidd and Jeanne L. Rivoire (Eds.). New York, Int. Univs., 1966.

14. Fantz, Robert L.: Pattern vision in young infants. *Psychol Rec. 8:43,* 1958.

16. Fleishman, Edwin A., and Ellison, Gaylor D.: A factor analysis of fine manipulative tests. *J Appl Psychol, 46:96,* 1962.

17. Fleishman, Edwin A.; Thomas, Paul, and Munroe, Philip: The dimensions of physical fitness—A factor analysis of speed, flexibility, balance and coordination tests. Technical Report No. 3, The Office of Naval Research Department of Industrial Administration and Department of Psychology, Yale University, New Haven, September 1961.

18. Haith, Marshall M.: The response of the human newborn to visual movement. *J Exp Child Psychol, 3:235,* 1966.

19. Harris, Laureen: The effects of relative novelty on children's choice behaviors. *J Exp Child Psychol, 2:297,* 1964.

20. Held, Richard, and Bossom, Joseph: Neonatal deprivation and adult rearrangement: Complementary techniques for analyzing plastic sensory-motor coordination. *J Comp Physiol Psychol, 54(1):33,* 1961.

21. Held, Richard, and Freedman, Sanford J.: Plasticity in human sensorimotor control. *Science, 142:455,* 1963.

22. Held, Richard: Plasticity in sensory-motor systems. *Sci Amer, 213(5):1,* 1965.

23. Hershenson, M.: *The Visual Preference Behavior of Newborn Infants* (unpublished Doctoral Dissertation). Yale University, 1964.

24. Howard, I. P., and Templeton, W. B.: *Human Spatial Orientation*. London, Wiley, 1966.

25. Judd, C. H.: Movement and consciousness. *Psychol Rev*, 7:199, 1905.

26. Kephart, Newell C.: *The Slow Learner in the Classroom*. Columbus, Ohio, E. Merrill, 1960.

27. Kidd, Aline H., and Rivoire, Jeanne L.: *Perceptual Development in Children*. New York, Int. Univs., 1966.

28. Kilpatrick, F.P.: Two processes in perceptual learning. *J Exp Psychol*, 36:187, 1946.

29. Leton, Donald A.: Visual-motor capacities and ocular efficiency in reading. *Percept Motor Skills*, 15:407, 1962.

30. Mendel, Giseld: Children's preferences for differing degrees of novelty. *Child Develop*, 36:452, 1966.

31. Roff, Merrill: A factorial study of tests in the perceptual area. *Psychometric Monogr*, 41:8, 1953.

32. Smith, Karl U.: *Cybernetic Principles of Learning and Educational Design*. New York, Holt, 1965.

33. Smith, O. W., and Smith, Patricia C.: Developmental studies of spatial judgments by children and adults. *Percept Motor Skills*, 22:3, 1966.

34. Smock, Charles D., and Holt, B. Gene.: Children's reactions to novelty: An experimental study of "curiosity motivation". *Child Develop*, 33:631, 1962.

35. Sokolov, E. N.: Neuronal models and the orienting reflex. In *Central Nervous System and Behavior*. M. A. B. Brazier (Ed.). New York, Macy Foundation, 1960.

36. Spears, W. C.: The assessment of visual discrimination and preference in the human infant (unpublished Doctoral Dissertation), Brown University, 1962.

37. Tinker, M. A.: The study of eye movement in reading. *Psychol Bull*, 43:93, 1946.

38. White, Burton L., and Held, Richard: Plasticity of sensorimotor development in the human infant. In *The Causes of Behavior: Readings in Child Development and Educational Psychology*. Judy F. Rosenblith and Wesley Allinsmith (Eds.). Boston, Allyn and Bacon, 1966.

39. Werner, Heinz, and Wapner, W.: Sensory-tonic field theory of perception. *J Personality*, 18:88, 1949.

40. Werner, Heinz; Wapner, W., and Chandler, K. A.: Experiments on sensory-tonic field theory of perception. II. Effect of supported and unsupported tilt of body on the visual perception of verticality. *J Exp Psychol*, 42:346, 1951.

TABLE I

THE EMERGENCE OF SELECTED PERCEPTUAL, MOTOR, AND PERCEPTUAL—MOTOR BEHAVIORS IN INFANTS FROM BIRTH TO TWO YEARS

	Visual-Perceptual	Motor	Perceptual-Motor
Birth 0	Visual regard, seeks novelty, is attracted by pattern, movement, birghtness Focal distance 7 1/2"		
30 days	Horizontal pursuit Vertical and circular pursuit Looks at hands	Lifts head and chest when prone	"Swipes" at objects
60 days	Convergence of eyes possible		
90 days	Observes fist and finger movements extensively	Can turn from back to side Hands frequently open Sits with support	Torso orients toward objects Reaches toward objects
	Visual accommodation comparable to adult capacity	Rolls from back to stomach	Contacts objects accurately with hands
6 months	Visually alert 50% of waking hours Visually pursues targets moving at wide range of speeds	Hand preference first emerges	Can hold two objects simultaneously
	Size discrimination	Raises to sitting position unaided	Opposes thumb in seeking cube
1 year		Hand preference when reaching continues	Locomotor reafferent behavior (walking with visual monitoring of movements)
18 months		Climbs stairs or chair	Scribbles imitatively
		Walks while visually attending to environment	Scribbles spontaneously
		Hand preference less distinct	Plays simple game of catch with ball
2 years	Form discrimination develops	Runs	Imitates vertical and horizontal strokes

B. Research Guidelines

Chapter 6

RESEARCH IN HUMAN MOVEMENT

RESEARCH has become a magic word in the twentieth century. It has been blamed for the tools of man's destruction while being praised for its contributions to science, technology, education and health. Research is speculation translated into action. It is the core of the scientific process, the preacher at the wedding of statistics and theory. Research involves the synthesis of previously unrelated observations presented in a logical manner in exact terms which others can understand. Research is not necessarily finding the answers to practical problems but thrives best in an atmosphere which permits the scientist to freely explore questions which are important to him.

Research is hard work; it begins with a theoretical position combined with a search of the library. It continues with the designing of a workable approach to a problem and the collection of data and terminates with an enumeration of all the questions which have been raised by the findings. Research involves breaking down categories. Often lines of demarcation established by various academic disciplines are crossed. A unique approach is discovered. Something new is created.

Research may be the "sinking of shafts" into unexplored problem areas or "piling pebbles" as previously investigated studies are examined more closely. Polling the attitudes of a physical education class, surveying a school district's needs, and delving into an esoteric ques-

A speech presented to the National Convention of the American Association for Health, Physical Education and Recreation at Dallas, Texas, March 20, 1965.

tion in the hallowed confines of the university laboratory will require sound research methodology. Research is thus an exploratory process of some new idea or thing and the translation of this sojourn into ideas which may underlie new theories or reinforce old ones, which may enhance practice, and which leads to further scientific exploration.

It seems to me that at the present time the future of physical education as an academic subject worthy of study at the university level, as well as its acceptability by secondary and elementary school administrators is largely dependent upon the manner in which we attempt to justify our practices and present a logical rationale for what we do *to* and *for* children. Futhermore, it seems apparent that sound research is at the core of this search for rationale. And while needed research of human movement seems without end, it is believed that the following three problem areas are in most need of scientific study by members of our profession.

1. *The social psychology of physical activity.* Although attention has been paid to the influence of the broad cultural-historical context upon human movement while at the same time physiological and psychological variables influencing the individual have been elucidated to some extent, largely missing has been an emphasis upon the influence of various sub-cultures surrounding the individual upon his selection of activities, his skill level, as well as his general inclination to participate.

   a. Influence of familial attitudes upon the fitness of children.

   b. The achievement of status in the peer group as a function of physical proficiency—a function of age, sex, or just what?

   c. The audience effect; the influence of negative and positive encouragement upon performance.

   d. Child-rearing practices and the movement capacities of children.

   e. The effect of ordinal position in the family upon movement skills.

2. *Movement as an affective experience.* Kephart,

Delacato, Harmon and Getman have suggested various theoretical models, combined with various clinical practices which purport to enhance verbal, perceptual, and auditory functioning through motor activities. It would be helpful to determine just what things they do in their program produce the changes they describe. Some of the specific problems which might be explored in this area include:

a. Does motor training enhance a general self-concept which may influence learning because of increased self-confidence or is specific training of a portion of the nervous system involved?

b. Is laterality related to directionality? and more important, is there a causal relationship between these two perceptual qualities?

c. To what extent does rapport between clinician and child and/or between mother and child overcome or enhance the value of activities carried on between them which purport to improve visual perception or neurological organization?

3. *The perceptual process.* Studies are needed of *why* people do what they do, not just what they do. The influence of judgments and meanings given to experience are as important to consider as what people do.

a. Developmental studies of kinesthetic perception; kinesthetic perception as a function of age.

b. The nature of visual-space perception; how movements in space are organized and more specifically, how people track balls they hope to intercept.

c. The objectification of the "self" concept as related to physical activities; the objective body, the performing self (aspiration level), as well as the total psycho-social self.

d. The effects of isolating input channels upon perceptions.

e. Perceptual distortions of kinesthetic senations and of movements in visual space and particularly the possible facilitation or hindrance of these distortions.

In conclusion, it is suggested that academic respectibility on the university campus as well as sound practices in the school districts will be enhanced to the extent to which logical rationale underlies practice. Failure to meet the other scientists and academicians in/on their own terms (scientific terms supported by evidence gained from sound research) could lead to our extinction.

Chapter 7

NEW PERSPECTIVES UPON MAN IN ACTION

$\mathbf{A}$ FIFTY-YEAR LAG has often been referred to as existing between the discovery of new knowledge and its application. I do not believe, however, that this delay is inevitable. With increased facilities at our disposal for communication plus the mobility of modern man, new knowledge is dispersed more quickly to individuals who can utilize it (1).

At this point critical problems arise because new knowledge about some facet of man or his environment implies that someone or some group of people should change, and the blocks to change are formidable. In addition to practical problems involving geography, facilities and money, in order for an individual in charge to make significant changes in a program, he has to admit that perhaps he has been doing something in the past which might be done differently in the future—an admission not everyone is willing to make.

Another problem is the determination of when "new knowledge" is really that, and not the result of some experimental "game" which bears little relationship to real situations and people. Experimenters must realize that all helpful practices in education are not necessarily amenable to exploration in the research laboratory while educators must realize that much of what they do could probably be carried out more effectively if subjected to experimental validation.

Research, carefully carried out, is helpful in separat-

Speech presented at the University of California at Santa Barbara, February 16, 1967.

ing fact from fancy. Within the conglomerate of research findings are trends which may prove helpful or at least interesting to the physical educator. Man is finding out more and more about man. And so, I would like to toss a multipronged pitchfork at you and bring to your attention areas of research which are becoming prominent and should be acted upon by individuals in physical education and related fields. We will discuss briefly findings of studies in the areas of social psychology, biochemistry, neuroanatomy, anthropology, and special education which have implications for man in action.

The literature in social psychology is replete with implications for the physical educator (2). Among the findings are those which relate to the following topics:

1. Developmental trends in the effect of an audience upon performance.

2. The nature of competition.

3. The assumption of gender in children.

4. The influence of affiliative needs versus achievement needs in groups upon their collective performance.

5. Need achievement in children as a function of child-rearing practices.

6. Leadership traits, onset of maturation, and physical prowess.

The research in biochemistry and neurophysiology of learning suggests that (5).

1. Man remembers everything!

2. Only indirect evidence that RNA and DNA have anything to do with learning.

3. Brain wave amplitude may influence receptivity of the nervous system.

4. Studies involving RNA injections in animals and humans have resulted in contradictory findings.

The anthropologist has difficulty carrying out his work because of the lack and variability of human and human-like remains. Recent evidence suggests that (5).

1. Components of the human action system evolved at different times.

2. Muscle use can cause remarkable changes in

structure to take place during a rather short period of time.

3. Man's unique function as an animal is caused by brain, manual and visual systems being highly associated and highly developed.

In our own laboratory and in other psychological laboratories it is being found that there are innumerable personal equations in movement (6):

1. Persistence seems a general factor.
2. Spatial qualities in movement have been identified.
3. Preferred speed and rhythm are also being investigated.
4. Preferences for forceful movement may also be general factors.

Evidence from the child development literature suggests that intermediate between inherent and learned facets of movement behavior lie actions which may be the result of a form of imprinting including the following (1):

1. Smiling in infants.
2. Gait, throwing and gesture patterns.
3. Gender identification in children.

Special educators have become concerned about various movement panaceas which have been offered by certain clinicians throughout the country through which it is claimed that a variety of perceptual, verbal, cognitive and sensory deficiencies in atypical children can be alleviated. Research evidence, however, suggests that

1. Perceptual-motor training programs deal with qualities which are related only to certain components of classroom functioning.
2. Laterality and cross-dominance may not be highly related to reading, writing or various other achievement tests.

Movement education programs are being established in the Los Angeles City Schools for special education with several purposes in mind (4).

It is believed that the physical educator, if he proves himself capable as a researcher or clinician, will be called upon more and more to combine with other members of the educational team who are attempting to improve the learning of both "normal" and atypical children. Similarly, others within university academic communities will continue to seek out those of us who prove ourselves capable researchers and scholars. It is believed that our contribution to research and education will come as the direct result of the following attitudes on our part:

1. We must not claim too much for the role of movement activities in education. To state that movement is the basis for the development of all cognition on the part of the child is to ignore a mountain of experimental evidence.

2. We must be prepared to demonstrate that observable human action can influence certain other components of the human personality and demonstrate this in objective terms acceptable to other researchers dealing with human behavior. To suggest that we are influencing man's "energy surround" or that we are interested in the interactions between man and his environment is to say very little. We must translate our feelings about reality into research designs which result in findings that others can understand.

To claim to be interested in everything is to tell others that we are incapable of understanding anything. Being interested in something does not infer that a scholarly attempt is being made to gain understanding. Philosophical speculations concerning the role of man in the culture, his place in society, and his unique features were acceptable in the 1930's. This kind of speculation, however, should be accompanied by the collection of hard data in the late 1960's.

REFERENCES

1. Brown, Roscoe, and Cratty, Bryant J. (Eds.): *New Perspectives of Men in Action.* Englewood Cliffs, Prentice-Hall, 1968 (in press).
2. Cratty, Bryant J.: *Social Dimensions of Physical Activity,* Englewood Cliffs, Prentice-Hall, 1967.
3. Cratty, Bryant J.: *Psychology and Physical Activity.* Englewood Cliffs, Prentice-Hall, 1967.

4. Cratty, Bryant J.: Perceptual-motor attributes of mentally retarded children and youth (Monogr.). Mental Retardation
Services Board of Los Angeles County, 1966.
5. Cratty, Bryant J.: Neurological and biochemical bases of learning
and retention (Chapt. 15). Personal equations in movement
(Chapt. 12). Evolution of the human action system (Chapt. 2).
Movement Behavior and Motor Learning, 2nd ed. Philadelphia,
Lea and F., 1967.
6. Cratty, Bryant J.: Perceptual thresholds of non-visual locomotion. Monogr. I and II, NIH Research, supported by the National
Institute of Neurological Diseases and Blindness, 1965, 1966.

C. Movement Activities in General Education

Chapter 8

THE USE AND MISUSE OF MOVEMENT IN EDUCATION

P ERCEPTUAL FUNCTIONING is being looked upon with increased interest by educators, special educators, psychiatrists and psychologists. "Positive" psychiatry is focused upon the obvious, the here and the now, one portion of which involves what a person can do motorically. How a child moves is a primary way in which he is judged by his peers. His general clumsiness may lead toward hostility as he frequently bumps his fellows in classrooms, while more specific ineptitudes prevent him from achieving success in games valued by his peers. Engaging a disturbed child in a ball game becomes a part of what has been termed *reality therapy.*

Special educators have begun to look upon movement experiences as possible channels through which a variety of sub-normal attributes of atypical children might be enhanced. Since intellect is manifested to a large extent through motor output, i.e. writing, often sub-par classroom performance is caused, not so much by the inability to mentally manipulate abstractions and symbols, but by the inability to express motorically the results of these mental processes on the printed page.

Progressive educators have for a long time postulated that a primary way in which male children achieve a feeling of identity and success is through their success in games. Failure to do this can result in a general rejection of the self which is reflected in poor performance in the classroom.

Speech to the Symposium on Motor Learning, November 1966, Milwaukee, Wisconsin.

Through the history of thought men have speculated that the stages through which the developing infant passes might be likened to the evolution of the race. This recapitulation theory was espoused by Rousseau as he suggested that children pass from the animal through the savage and pastoral stages until they reach the social stage which culminates in their marriage to the ideal girl.

Clinicians in some parts of the country working with brain-injured children have also begun to base practices upon the assumption that otogeny parallels phylogeny. Reconstructing the stages in the motor development of atypical children, it is sometimes assumed, will result in a kind of reorganization of the damaged neural structures which will remedy other functions purportedly mediated by the same structures (3).

This approach to ameliorating the problems of the brain-damaged child has received a great amount of public attention in recent years for several seasons. The theoretical underpinnings are easy to understand and present a reasonably logical explanation of brain damage, its causes and effects. Parents of children with mild to profound cerebral dysfunctions are given simple techniques which they can apply themselves, thus relieving to some extent their own tensions and guilt. Professional workers in disciplines dealing with cerebral function and motor activities have generally failed to present to educators and parents constructive alternatives to the techniques arising from this recapitulation theory. Proponents of this theory seem adroit at exploiting their ideas by gaining maximum coverage in popular magazines and newspapers.

The simple motor sequences proposed by advocates of the recapitulation theory *are* helpful to brain-damaged children with mild to severe neurological dysfunction. The child who is severely handicapped because of some kind of neurological impairment may be particularly helped by practice of some of the simple motor activities proposed by these clinicians.

Children who are neurologically handicapped are hampered by an excess of unspecific residual muscular tensions. Some of the patterning advocated, as well as the crawling and creeping, may aid in alleviating this kind of inappropriate tension.

Youths with brain dysfunction usually exhibit the inability to coordinate movements of the left and right of the body and also fail to coordinate well the upper part of the body and the lower part. Basic locomotor training helps to alleviate this kind of motor problem. Basic work in crawling, creeping, and walking has always been included in programs of therapy for neurologically handicapped children.

It is believed, however, that these theorists are vulnerable to scientific scrutiny when they propose that attempting to establish hemispheric dominance through selected unilateral activities will somehow aid in the improvement of speech, audition, and other perceptual and conceptual functions of the normal as well as of the brain-injured child. There is no direct evidence that engaging in a few motor activities will have any effect upon the central nervous system of either retarded or normal youngsters. Claiming that the intellect of modern man will be improved by primarily engaging in unilateral behaviors is an even more tenuous supposition; ape men living about three million years ago, possessing a brain one-third the size of ours, exhibited the tendency to utilize their right hands in unilateral activities (bashing out the brains of unsuspecting baboons).

The human nervous system was looked upon by the neurologists of the 1800's and 1900's as composed of simple laminations from the lower centers controlling the more basic functions to the higher ones mediating intellect, speech, and the like. After the turn of the century, however, more sophisticated studies of the human brain became possible with the advent of increased knowledge in biochemistry and electronics. The primary finding was that the brain was an extremely complex instrument mediating human behavior by the nearly simultaneous interactions of innumerable portions. Vertical integrating systems as well as horizontal layers of neural tissue participate "in concert" to produce fluid verbal and perceptual-motor acts (6).

Even the neat maps denoting the portions of the motor cortex purporting to control certain muscle groups became suspect when experimenters found that placing an electrode on a small portion of the motor cortex would at first elicit a twitching of one muscle group, but if continued would later elicit the flexion of another (6).

Electrical stimulation of various portions of the cortex would produce only unspecific writhings of muscles; the smoothing of muscle action seemed to depend upon the integration of other more basic structures including the reticular action system, the cerebellum, and the medulla (6).

With such findings available to us in the neurological literature, the assumption that single and discrete portions of the brain control complex motor acts like crawling and creeping is somewhat naive. The hypothesis that crawling or creeping will somehow improve other functions mediated by the same portions of the brain controlling these motor acts becomes even less tenable. Crawling involves almost the entire nervous system and seems to improve little but crawling.

Despite the miraculous improvement claimed for children subjected to these programs there is an increasing number of well-controlled scientific studies which make one further skeptical of this kind of neural lamination theory. Robbins, for example, not only found that extensive programs of creeping and crawling failed to elicit improvement in scores elicited from standardized perceptual, reading and achievement tests, but also found that no improvement in laterality was forthcoming after engaging in these types of activities (5).

Others have put forth theories of perceptual-motor education which do not assume that the central nervous system will undergo marked and rapid change after engaging in simple locomotor acts. These more peripheral theories suggest practices which are more comprehensive and include a variety of tasks emphasizing balance, body-image training, agility, and various kinds of activities involving hand-eye coordination (4).

Proponents of both types of theories are having a

marked effect upon special education, an effect which is hopefully encouraging some to look more closely at the total child in action on the playfield, to observe how he moves and the effects of his movement accuracy upon his social acceptance, upon his ability to express his intellectual functioning through handwriting, and upon his ability to organize his world visually. Many school districts throughout the country are more and more incorporating motor activities as means through which the retarded and the neurologically handicapped will be helped to learn.

Perceptual-motor activities are not magical panaceas through which all the global and profound problems of handicapped children can be improved. I believe, however, that these kinds of activities, if properly applied, can have a greater impact upon the learning of normal and atypical children than was believed possible in the past. Programs of fitness exercises and the provision of time for the teaching of sports skills have a far-reaching effect upon the social and physical development of children (2). There are additional programs of movement activities, however, which can have an even more important influence upon primary school children, as well as upon the retarded and neurologically handicapped child.

For the past year I have spent one day a week as a consultant to the Special Education Branch of the Los Angeles City Schools. I believe that my hiring was in part attributable to the emergence of the theoretical positions described previously. During this year I have visited schools of special education, conducted teachers' institutes, and in other ways have attempted to outline programs of motor activities which will improve various components of classroom learning, as well as sequences of tasks which are designed to improve a wide range of perceptual-motor attributes. Data upon which some of these practices have been based have been obtained from our research at the University and from research conducted for the Los Angeles County Mental Retardation Services Board with whom I have worked as a consultant (1).

These programs have several dimensions. One of the primary points we emphasize involves the gradual emancipation of the children from control by the teacher to controls evolved by the children themselves. This dimension will be vividly portrayed tomorrow by Dr. Mosston, so we will not take the time here to elaborate upon it.

There are other dimensions to the program we propose. Essentially, we suggest to the teachers that the child be exposed to a variety of perceptual-motor activities and that these be presented in an approximate order dictated by their difficulty, including tasks designed to enhance balance, agility, manual skill, ball handling ability, and the like. Emphasis is placed upon requiring the children to integrate vision with movement, to jump into squares or over lines, not simply to jump; to creep while placing their hands into red hand-prints on the floor, not simply to creep in a disorganized and random fashion.

It is believed that children should be well motivated when they perform, that they should not simply be treated like animals and made to perform a few simple tasks. It is further suggested that extremely basic activities should be incorporated in the program. Balance, for example, should begin with static postures on the mat; jumping and skipping should be begun with the simple attempt to swing the arms rhythmically, while body-image training should start by asking the child to identify the large planes of the body, i.e. his front, side, and back.

The teachers are further encouraged to develop their own sequences of activities or to further refine the sequences presented to them by conducting action research within their classrooms. Such sequences are reasonably easy to derive by asking all the members of a class to perform a variety of tasks involving agility, for example, and then by ascertaining the percentage capable of performing various ones, and finally by arranging the tasks in order of difficulty from the simplest to the more taxing.

In addition to these basic developmental sequences, the playgrounds within the schools are undergoing a change. Strange configurations are appearing composed of orange lines zigzagging in all directions. The teachers are being encouraged to explore gross movement of the total body as a helpful learning modality accompanying the channels of sensory input utilized in the classroom (vision, hearing, tactual exploration).

These tasks are not presented as the only way to teach the trainable retardate to read, but are suggested as simply another but important avenue through which to reach children with defective nervous systems, as well as children in the primary grades whose nervous systems are in some ways similar.

If a child is to recognize a letter, he must recognize basic shapes. Letters are composed of triangles, half-circles, squares, rectangles, and various combinations of these shapes. If a child cannot distinguish between a square and a rectangle he cannot be expected to identify letters. Playgrounds formerly containing only the traditional circles and squares are now appearing painted with triangles, half-circles and the like. Thus children now first attempt to identify these shapes in a classroom, go to the playground and try to locate their counterparts, then play on these shapes, walk around them, and in other ways interact with these larger representations of basic spatial configurations. Following this, the children may return to the classroom, where letters are made from the basic shapes; triangles become A's while half-circles become C's and with the addition of a straight line, a B.

Returning to the playground the children now find grids composed of squares about one foot by one foot in size into which letters have been placed. By hopping or otherwise traveling into these squares the children may enhance their ability to spell. Similar grid patterns containing numerals are also being used to aid in the teaching of simple quantitative concepts.

Spelling, however, requires other intellectual attributes. To spell *cat* one must remember three things in a series, *c*, *a*, and *t* must be placed in order, and this order must be remembered if the word is later to be dealt with correctly. Again I proposed an activity on the playground which might be helpful in the ability to order things in a series.

Two-dimensional obstacle courses also have been inscribed on the asphalt. These other configurations consist of a line ending in a circle, followed by a zigzag line, etc. The children attempt to negotiate one, then two, then three or more of these in order. They try to remember the order, or try to remember the manner in which they or their classmates decide to travel over them. If the child cannot remember two tasks in a given order involving his entire body in action, it is extremely doubtful if he can be expected to arrange letters in a desired order when spelling. At the same time the extent to which a child evidences the ability to order things in a series when acting out these kind of movement tasks is instantly apparent to the observing teacher, far more obvious than attempting to determine why the child is confused or accurate as he flicks his eyes across the printed page while seated at a desk.

In a similar manner it is being attempted to "slow down" the hyperactive child. Movement tasks are presented to them which require performance over increasing periods of time. Line-walking is requested and the length of the line gradually increased. The failure of the hyperactive child to focus on a task is again more apparent to the teacher when the task involves gross movement than when the child is seated at a desk. Similarly, evaluating improvement in the ability of the child to place himself under his own control becomes apparent using this kind of task. One of the fallacies perpetrated upon special educators by physical educators is the hoary "drainage theory" which suggests that hyperactivity can somehow be "used up" by having the child engage in vigorous and physically taxing motor activities. The effects of this approach upon the emotional stability and activity level of the brain-injured child are usually disastrous.

Hyperactivity in children may be reduced only if they are engaged in tasks which elicit sustained concentration and interest. Attempting to reduce hyperactivity in children by introducing frantic physical activity is a little like attempting to reduce the tensions of the sex pervert by permitting him to view pornographic pictures.

There are further dimensions to the program we are introducing into the schools. One of the pressing problems of many young boys and girls from four to ten years of age is the development of behaviors which stamp them as identifying with the appropriate gender.

After several years during which I evaluated boys brought to me for skill problems, it was found that their main problems actually revolved around their attempts to "find themselves" as young males. I began to delve into the literature and to question experts about gender identification in children and related problems in adults (2).

Dr. Evelyn Hooker, one of the nation's leading authorities on male homosexuality, began our conversation with the exclamation, "I was wondering if anyone in physical education would ever call me!!!" This was followed shortly by the news that "70 percent of the male homosexuals I interview cite their confrontation with physical activities as a critical turning point in their development. They attempted to perform, failed to do well and either retreated into companionship with other poor performing males or began to play with the girls. These men report to me that they actively sought help in this form of masculine expression, but when failing to get it began to develop other modes of behavior inappropriate to boys." While the causes of homosexuality are devious and subtle, and certainly more complex than simply the inability to play games well, the statements by Dr. Hooker certainly hold important implications for physical educators and denote an important use of perceptual-motor activities in the total educational process.

There are innumerable other uses of motor training in education. Extensive programs of manual dexterity emphasizing tasks to heighten the perception of the hands would certainly assist many children who are having difficulty writing. Body-image training would seem important in helping retarded and neurologically handicapped children to organize themselves and their surroundings more effectively. In recent studies a correlation of .8 was found between a body-image score and scores obtained from retarded children on a variety of perceptual-motor tasks involving balance, agility, ball skills and the like (1). Similarly it was also found recently that a perfect correlation existed between tasks designed to evaluate perception of the hands, and manual dexterity. Thus both body-image and "hand-image" seem intimately connected to the ability to *move* the body and the hands accurately.

We have perhaps slighted motor education of the traditional nature intended to improve sports skills. But we should not. It is enough to place emphasis on basic motor activities for no other reason than to improve a child's self-image as he engages in games. A large portion of a boy's self-concept between the ages of five and fifteen hinges on whether he can perform well in socially approved games. The late-maturing male has been found to be traditionally lacking in self-confidence and in similar measures primarily due to his inability to perform well in skills approved by his peer group (2).

In summary, therefore, we believe that perceptual-motor activities offer no magic solution to many of the profound problems of the retarded and otherwise neurologically impaired children. At the same time, if intelligently applied, these kinds of tasks can offer help in certain components of classroom learning, in the formation of basic perceptions necessary to reading and writing, as well as in aiding the retarded child to think in a more organized fashion, in helping the hyperactive child to place himself under control, in helping the male child to express his maleness and the female to manifest her femininity, and in improving the general self-concept of all children.

The answer to the complex problems of complex children as they attempt to carry out the judgments required of them in a complex world is not to ask them to crawl on the floor. A study of the nineteenth century neurologists offers fascinating insights into the background of man's quest for knowledge about the human brain; but the knowledge gained from these searchings should not dictate practices designed to "neurologically organize" children in the twentieth centruy.

A student of mine last year asked me, after attempting to reconcile the apparently contradictory research findings relating to the perceptual-motor functioning of humans, "What is the key to understanding this material?" The answer I gave to her I give to you now: Humans are complex; they function in complex ways, and their behavior fluctuates due to the impingement of a large variety of variables. Learn all you can; then be prepared to change your mind when new evidence is forthcoming. To understand this complexity, however, one should not retreat to the false security of archaic simplicities.

REFERENCES

1. Cratty, Bryant J.: The perceptual-motor attributes of mentally retarded children and youth (Monogr.). Mental Retardation Services Board of Los Angeles County, August 1966.
2. Cratty, Bryant J.: *Social Dimensions of Physical Activity.* Englewood Cliffs, Prentice-Hall, 1967.
3. Delacato, Carl H.: *The Diagnosis and Treatment of Speech and Reading Problems.* Springfield, Thomas, 1963.
4. Kephart, Newell C.: *The Slower Learner in the Classroom.* Columbus, Ohio, C. E. Merrill, 1963.
5. Robbins, Melvyn Paul: The Delacato interpretation of neurological organization. *Reading Res Quart, Spring:*59, 1966.
6. Wooldridge, Dean E.: *The Machinery of the Brain.* New York, McGraw-Hill, 1963.

Chapter 9

EGO GROWTH AND MOVEMENT EFFICIENCY

FREUD DEFINED the ego *as a vehicle connecting the underlying personality with the real world of experience.* A detailed examination of Freud's works, however, indicates that importance was attached to movement primarily as a means to assess the unconscious. For example, in one of his case studies it is stated:

If the lips are silent he chatters with his finger tips, betrayal oozes out of him at every pore. And thus the task of making conscious the most hidden recesses of the mind is one which is quite possible to accomplish (Fragment of an analysis of a case of hysteria. In *Collected Papers,* III. London, Hogarth Press, 1933).

It is believed that Lewinian field theory presents a conceptual framework which emphasizes the importance of perceptual-motor behavior to the total psychosocial "*self*." Lewin suggests that the perceptual-motor region acts as the buffer between the individual's "inner personal region" and his total "life space." It is suggested that interactions between the individual's self and his social-cultural environment is facilitated, modified, and otherwise influenced by his perceptual-motor behavior.

When attempting to relate and discuss factors which are important to the development of the child's ego, it is important to ask what kind of evidence forms the primary means through which his self is constructed. Through what kind of behavior can others best judge, react to, and inter-

Speech given to the Second Annual Conference for Teachers, San Fernando Valley State College, March 6, 1965. Sponsored by the Los Angeles County and City Schools, the San Fernando Child Guidance Clinic, The Laurence School, and the San Fernando Valley Mental Health Association.

act with him? Is the child to himself what he thinks, what he does, what he says or just what? It is believed that an important kind of behavior upon which the child judges himself, and upon which others may judge him as an individual involves movement; and therefore the worth of the self is to some extent dependent upon the efficiency with which the child moves.

It seems to me that there are at least six contexts in which perceptual-motor behavior assumes importance as the child forms his self concept.

1. Rather early in life the infant's primary means of expression of communication and of learning involves movement. Early manipulatory experience and attempts at locomotion are primary means through which the child's worth and intelligence are judged. Exploratory behavior is an initial means through which the child learns shapes, sizes, distances, and other concepts in his life space. Although as he grows older other kinds of behavior (social, verbal etc.) begin to assume increasing importance in his life, motor tasks remain an important means through which his development is assessed. Walking is followed by learning to ride a bicycle, and later dancing—all motor tasks. Thus, movement inefficiency can prove a detriment as the child begins to explore and to learn about his world, creating perceptual lags which will interfere with a healthy self-concept from the initial months of life.

2. Movement is important because it involves the primary means through which others judge the child. No one can see him think; everyone can see him move. And as he is seen he is reacted to, either positively or negatively, and in turn reacts to and evaluates these reactions. It is believed that the social feedback to the child's motor behaviors is a primary means by which his worth or unworthiness is assessed.

3. Movement is an important adjunct to verbal communication, and movements form a mode of communication in their own right. Verbal communication is enhanced to the extent to which appropriate facial expressions, effective gesture patterns, and posturings of the total body

accompany word symbols. It is reasonable, therefore, to assume that communication between the child and his peers, family and others with whom he comes in contact will be impeded if his movements are clumsy.

4. An important way through which social interaction may take place is in culturally approved sports and games. Inefficiency in perceptual-motor functioning makes the child a less desirable social "animal," blunts his inclination to interact with others, and may add impetus to the child's withdrawal from his peers. Unworthiness in games, to a boy to whom this kind of behavior has been judged culturally important, can result in a rather total rejection of himself in other areas of behavior or can lead to other undesirable kinds of compensations: withdrawal into professorial behavior at the age of ten, continual attention-getting comedy, or a rather total withdrawal from all kinds of learning situations.

5. Motor efficiency is particularly important to the ego construction of the boy in our culture. Effective participation in sports and games is a primary means by which his manhood is proved to himself and to others. It is behavior which best distinguishes boys from girls in our society—vigorous participation in large muscle activities. Therefore, if a boy is deficient in perceptual-motor skills, it seems safe to assume that his total self-concept will be marred; negative feedback is received from his peers, and from his father as he seeks to demonstrate his emerging manliness.

6. Movement and the inclination to move in rather vigorous ways provide important means of relieving tension. Thus an individual who perceives his movements and perhaps his body as unsightly, and thus does not engage in vigorous movements, loses an important avenue through which to relieve situationally engendered tensions. Notable during finals at the University is the great upsurge in participation in our recreational activities, as students instinctively seek to relieve tensions on the playing fields produced by academic pressures.

To summarize, it seems that deficiencies in movement capacities and skills result in several kinds of impairments which reflect upon the ego growth of the child. Physical development is impeded, and perceived inability is followed by disinclination to participate followed by a further lowering of capacity. Physiological effects include an impediment in early learning, a failure to demonstrate activities approved by the culture which purport to demonstrate manliness, as well as increased tension arising from a failure to dispel various biochemical products of stress. The social implications of movement inefficiency include a lessening of the opportunity to engage in social interaction as well as negative social feedback, which further lowers the child's self-concept.

Remedial measures involve breaking into the chain of events which has lowered the child's self-concept— counteracting negative experiences with satisfying ones. Training in a variety of movement capacities which underlie sports skills is imperative; balance, agility, strength, endurance, as well as the specifics of various athletic sports may be improved if individual attention is given to the child in relatively non-threatening situations.

It seems to me that in most elementary schools, interested male and female teachers might institute special classes which attempt to enhance the capacities of children whose movements are inefficient. It is believed important that we consider the total individual in action, not only his hands with which he writes or his head with which he thinks. If his self-concept is formed to a marked degree by how society reacts to his actions, it seems to me that improving the appearance and efficiency of these actions warrants important consideration.

Chapter 10

THE GENDER IDENTIFICATION OF CHILDREN

IN ADDITION to acquiring genetic-biologic determinants of sex, as he begins life the child assumes a social-psychological gender. It is generally assumed that this latter type of identification is determined primarily by various environmental conditions with which the child is confronted during the formative years. There is evidence that gender acquisition begins rather early and is reflected almost immediately in the kinds of movement behavior which a child exhibits.

It is believed that this general problem area is of importance to the kinesiologist for two primary reasons: (a) There is a significant amount of clinical evidence suggesting that inappropriate early sex-role identification on the part of the child leads to adjustment problems in later life. One authority has stated that 70 percent of adult male deviates, subjected to a depth interview, mentioned the rejection by their peers when they attempted to assume a vigorous male role in game situations as a significant turning point in their early history. Deviates reported actively seeking help to improve their skills, and upon being rejected, reverting to friendships with other boys who evidenced similar inappropriate feminine behaviors. Thus in the clinical setting, opportunities exist for kinesiologists together with the child psychiatrist and psychologist to aid individual children having this kind of adjustment problem. Several authorities have suggested that specific tutoring in sex-appropriate skills is helpful in the treatment of children who have assumed an inappropriate sex-role. (b) Opportunities also exist for kinesiologists in research teams consisting of psychiatrists and psychologists to make a significant contribution to the knowledge about the assumption of appropriate gender behavior by male and female children. Initial studies should probably concern themselves with the construction of tools which would reliably identify movement characteristics which reflect a masculine or feminine component in personality. The validity of these might be established by correlating them with scores obtained by administering the tests constructed by Brown, Sutton-Smith and others.

The literature supports the following basic assumptions relative to this problem area:

1. There is less social stigma attached to masculinity in girls and women than to feminine behavior of boys.

2. There is an increasing tendency for girls in the United States to select the more vigorous activities formerly characteristic primarily of boys.

3. Physique type or hormonal characteristics are not generally predictive of the assumption of an inappropriate sex role in adulthood.

4. The passive male and active male may be differentiated early in life; a boy's characteristic method of behaving is reflected later in adolescence and early adulthood. It is found, for example, that boys in nursery school who use play materials vigorously, who are physically active, and who are "well-coordinated" tend to continue dominant and aggressive male behavior into adolescence and early adulthood. On the other hand, boys who are noted to be passive during their play, between the ages of three and six, and are reinforced in this behavior by their mothers, tend to select occupations which are primarily intellectual, are less aggressive in their initial sexual overtures to young women, and generally evidence less masculine behavior in later life.

5. Game choice has proved to be a valid and reliable means by which male-female roles may be differentiated in children.

6. Appropriate identification by boys is made difficult

in contemporary American society by the lack of opportunity for exposure to male models.

7. Parental characteristics which purportedly lead to the adoption of an inappropriate gender identification by both girls and boys is a unit containing a mother who is dominant and a father who is rejecting, ineffectual or absent.

8. There do not seem to be marked social class differences with regard to the assumption of inappropriate sex-role identification; however, this behavior is punished more in lower and middle-class homes than in upper-class homes.

9. Boys having only sisters tend to be more feminine in their choices of activities than do boys with only brothers. With spacing up to four years, second-born boys with older sisters tend to be more feminine than are the first-born with younger sisters.

10. Some authorities suggest that gender preference is the result of faulty "human imprinting" occurring early in the life of the infant.°

11. Early indices of inappropriate gender identification in children include persistent attempts to dress in clothes of the opposite sex; the display of gestures and mannerisms of the opposite sex; preference for games of the opposite sex; and at times the stated preference to be a member of the opposite sex.

It is instantly apparent to an individual observing a child with this problem that there is something "wrong" with the movement behaviors that are emitted. It is also clear that the manner in which the child moves is many times only a surface index of underlying maladjustment; however, *it is to these signs that the child's peers react, and it is these outward indices which elicit punishment from the child's social contacts.*

These inappropriate behaviors, however, are many times subtle and complex. For example, the writer re-

---

° Imprinting is a kind of learning triggered early in the life of an animal by a specific kind of perceptual event. The type of event may only vary within given limits.

cently participated in a diagnostic session at which a boy eleven years old who evidenced definite feminine behavior was brought into the room. It was interesting to note that each professional person present noticed a different aspect of the child's behavior which transmitted feminity. The speech therapist suggested that his voice was "too high"; the physical educators saw gross problems relative to the use of space when throwing, walking and running; the psychologists became concerned with subtle facial cues (he "talked too much" with his eyes, etc.); while the psychiatrists present reported still other indices.

It is believed that it is important for kinesiologists working with physical education major students to make them aware of this problem in children and to acquaint them of their potentially important role in aiding these children to readjust to an appropriate gender preference. Without passing moral judgment upon whether adult homosexuality is "good" or "bad," it is apparent that children who evidence behavior which is inappropriate to their biological sex have rather severe adjustment problems in childhood.

The problem is a complex one. However, it is believed that clinical and experimental kinesiologists with the aid of the child psychiatrist have the potential to make important inroads leading to new knowledge in this area. Programs might be instituted which could deal directly with the problem during early childhood. While it is difficult to envision how these programs might be implemented (it is probably not desirable for a group of these children to be brought together), it is believed that such a clinical environment might be operative at several levels. The children could be taught in a rather direct way the various skills appropriate to games in which a member of their sex usually participates. On the other hand, gesture patterns when eating, methods of walking, throwing, running, and similar basic activities might be transmitted to the child in a systematic way, perhaps with the use of film analyses or perhaps video-tape feedback. The literature generally indicates that individuals do not have an accurate perception of their *own* movement patterns.

Perhaps by such vivid portrayals the children might become more aware of how they are "different" and why they are not accepted by their peers.

At another less obvious level, the instructors in such a program should be made aware of the propensity on the part of children to imitate the behavior and movements of those with whom they come in contact. Thus administrators and instructors of such programs should be cognizant of the importance of transmitting a female or male movement pattern when working directly with these children.

References in the literature pertaining to the problem under discussion are appearing with more frequency. The problem of gender identification is an important one. The opportunity for service by kinesiologists is readily apparent; the opportunities for research limitless!

REFERENCES

1. Brim, O. G., Jr.: Family structure and sex role learning by children: A further analysis of Helen Koch's data. *Sociometry, 21*:1, 1958.
2. Brown, D. G.: Sex role preferences in young children. *Psychol Monogr, 70*:14, 1956.
3. Brown, D. G.: Masculinity-femininity development in children. *J Consult Psychol, 21*:197, 1957.
4. Cratty, Bryant J.: *Social Dimensions of Physical Activity.* Englewood Cliffs, Prentice-Hall, 1967.
5. Garai, Josef Ernest: Formation of the concept of "self" and development of sex identification. In *Perceptual Development in Children,* Aline H. Kidd and Jeanne L. Rivoire (Eds.). New York, Int. Univs., 1966.
6. Green, Richard, and Money, J.: Effeminacy in prepubertal boys: Summary of eleven cases and recommendations for case management. *Pediatrics, 27*(2):286, 1961.
7. Green, Richard, and Money, J.: Tomboys and sissies. *Sexology, 28*(5), 1961.
8. Kagan, Jerome: Personality, behavior and temperament. In *Human Development.* Frank Falkner (Ed.), Philadelphia, Saunders, 1966.
9. Koch, H. L.: Sissiness and tomboyishness in relation to sibling characteristics. *J Genet Psychol, 88*:231, 1956.
10. Maccoby, Eleanor E. (Ed.): *Development of Sex Differences.* Stanford, Stanford/Press, 1966.

11. Mussen, P., and Distler, L.M.: Masculinity identification and father-son relationships. *J Abnorm Soc Psychol, 59:*350, 1959.
12. Rosenberg, B. G., and Sutton-Smith, B.: Measurement of masculinity and femininity in children. *Sociometry, 22:*185,1959.
13. Rosenberg, B. G., and Sutton-Smith, B.: A revised conception of masculine-feminine differences in play activities. *J Genet Psychol, 104:*259, 1963.
14. Rosenberg, B. G., Sutton-Smith, B., and Morgan, E.: Use of opposite sex scales as a measure of psychosexual deviancy. *J Consult Psychol, 25:*221, 1961.
15. Sollenberger, R. T.: Some relationships between the urinary excretion of male hormone by maturing boys and their expressed interests and attributes. *J Psychol, 9:*179, 1940.
16. Sutton-Smith, B., and Rosenberg, B. G.: Impulsivity and sex preference. *J Genet Psychol, 98:*187, 1961.
17. Sutton-Smith, B., and Rosenberg, B. G.: Age changes in the effects of ordinal position on sex role identification. *J Genet Psychol, 107:*61, 1965.
18. Sutton-Smith, B., and Rosenberg, B. G.: Development of sex differences in play choice during pre-adolescence. *Child Develop, 34:*119, 1963.

Chapter 11

PERSONALITY IN MOVEMENT

IT HAS BECOME apparent within recent years that there is a collection of sub-surface qualities influential of motor performance and motor learning scores obtained in the laboratory which are relatively independent of directions extended by the experimenter. It is also probable that these same factors mold the performance and learning of skills in the less structured situations found on the playing field and gymnasium. This category of variables might be termed *individual preferences, personal equations,* or perhaps *individual biases in movement.* It seems probably that these personal equations are somewhat independent of the various indices of maximum capacity. Essentially they seem to be the outcome of the instructions a performer gives *himself* prior to starting a task—instructions of which the performer might not be aware.

These personal equations may be classified in several ways, but for the purposes of this discussion have been labelled *Task Persistence, Personal Rhythm, Preferred Speed,* and *Extent Preference.* To these might be added *Suggestibility* which refers to the extent to which a performer is influenced by directions from another when he acts.

Some experimental kinesiologists may suggest that these concepts are not amenable to treatment in a *scientific* manner, as they seem closely related to such vague problem areas as "expressive movement," "personality and movement," etc. It is believed, however, that inspection of the material which follows might convince the reader not only of the importance of these ideas, but also should suggest experimental approaches which might be utilized to explore these variables in rather exact ways.

TASK PERSISTENCE

Various researchers within the past forty years have attempted to determine whether a general or unitary quality termed *persistence* is present in a variety of perceptual-motor tasks. Although much of the work has not been of a high quality, the study by MacArthur in 1951 seems to point to the existence of a general persistence factor (12). Intercorrelating twenty-two measures of persistence, and parceling out intellectual differences, a simple factor analysis revealed that a general persistence factor did exist. More specifically MacArthur's analysis revealed this factor was reflected in scores obtained in a group of physical tasks including holding the foot over a chair, time of holding breath, maintained hand-grip, and arm extension. Ryans and Crutcher have also identified a general persistence factor (15,5). Thornton has isolated a general factor which he describes as "ability and/or willingness to withstand discomfort in order to achieve a goal" with high loadings in "time holding breath," "time standing still," "maintained hand-grip" and in similar tasks (16). Rethlingshafer also isolated a factor described as "willingness and/or ability to endure discomfort" (13).

Although the writer is unaware of studies relating such measures to vital capacity, it is apparent that such a factor could be an important variable when conducting experiments involving repetitive movements which lead to some degree of stress. Typical of the technique utilized when evaluating this quality is to first obtain maximum capacity (i.e. grip strength), ask the subject to maintain 50 percent to 75 percent maximum pressure, and then clock the duration of time he is willing to do this. In common with the other equations described in this discussion it is usually important to imbed such tasks within other groups of tasks so that the subjects are not aware of the purposes of the experiment

The possibilities of research within this problem area seem limitless. Determining whether persistence is a predictor of "courage," or of sustained performance in a variety of tasks and athletic contests would seem of paramount importance. In intellectual tasks a factor emerges which might be termed "persistence caused by social pressure" (12). Thus persistence in physical tasks as a function of social facilitation might also be investigated.

PERSONAL RHYTHM

Investigations supporting the existence of a general factor of personal rhythm are at the present time lacking. Studies by Lewis, Harding, and others have presented inconclusive findings (11,8). In general such a quality is obtained by analyzing the speed an individual selects when confronted with such unstructured directions as "tap rhythmically." It has also been found that most of the previous studies were handicapped by a scarcity of subjects and relatively unsophisticated statistical treatment of the data. Additional work in this area would initially require the identification of a simple factor structure using scores obtained by contrasting measures of total bodily rhythms; foot tapping, finger and hand tapping, etc., together with various neurophysiological measures including heart rate, resting respiration rate, together with scores obtained from various tests of steadiness carried out with several body parts.

The relation between some kinds of habitual personal rhythms and the ability to duplicate beats of various speeds emitted from music is also an area of investigation which holds promise.

PREFERRED SPEED

Relatively few investigations were carried out prior to the 1950's exploring the concept of "preferred speed." An investigation by Harrison and Dovens in 1938 produced findings which suggested that preferred speed of movement was highly specific (9). However, Kennedy and Travis in 1947 found a unitary speed factor present in the scores obtained when scores from a number of tasks were contrasted. Frischeisen-Kohler also suggested that a unitary speed factor existed, based upon preferred rates on tapping and metronome tests (7). Further evidence relating to question of whether a unitary factor exists indicative of the speed at which an individual habitually moves was presented in the factorial study by Rimoldi carried out in 1951. Utilizing fifty-nine measures of preferred speed and being careful not to suggest that performance speed was required, Rimoldi found that *habitual* motor speed was not related to speed elicited when individuals perform non-motor tasks (i.e. reading literature, reading news, etc. were included in the battery). Two separate motor factors emerged relative to preferred speed; one factor composed of test scores from tasks involving rhythmic movements and tapping movements, and a second factor composed of scores from tasks which required rather exact movements of the limbs (i.e. parallel movement of the legs while seated, etc.) (14).

In general, therefore, the evidence on the existence of a unitary speed factor based upon preferred speeds in various tasks is somewhat inconclusive. Absent are factorial studies in which tasks involving movement speed as a capacity measure have been included. Thus the relationships between movement speed as preferred and movement speed elicited when "speed stress" is experimentally induced are not known.

A survey of the literature on this question suggests several avenues to pursue. The influence of training for speed upon habitual speed would seem important to investigate. Movement speed as a function of general hyperactivity on the part of brain-damaged children, as well as the influence of various drugs upon habitual speed, and capacity for speed; all are important questions which require experimental treatment.

EXTENT PREFERENCE

Although early observers suggested the existence of

a general spatial factor present in unstructured movement tasks (1), the experimental designs with which this "aerial" quality has been explored leave much to be desired. More recently, however, evidence from several sources seems to indicate that there is a preferred distance which individuals prefer to move their arms and total bodies despite experimental instructions.

Bartley, for example, reviews an investigation which found that when individuals are to draw a line four inches in length, they tend to draw a longer one; conversely, people resist drawing a line which is fifteen inches in length when instructed to do so (2). Similarly, in a recently completed study by Cratty and Williams, blindfolded and earplugged subjects when asked to execute facing movements of 90, 180 and 360 degrees, overturned 90-degree or "quarter" turns by about 7 degrees, while underturning 180 and 360-degree turns by about 10 to 20 degrees, respectively (4). There seems to be a given amount of turning individuals *like* to do (somewhere between 90 and 180 degrees) just as there seems to be a preferred length of line people *like* to draw despite instructions extended by an experimenter.

These findings are rather intriguing. A simple factorial analysis might explore this phenomenon. The extent to which preferred extent of movement correlates with various personality measures has long been speculated upon in the experimental literature; however, relatively little objective work has been carried out on this question. The Figure Reconstruction Test devised by Brengelmann is perhaps the most exact experimental tool available with which to evaluate this elusive quality (3).

GENERAL CONSIDERATIONS

Needless to say, the exploration of some of these personal equations must proceed from a sound experimental orientation, and careful instruction of the subjects is also called for. Participants in these kinds of investigations must remain naive of the experimenter's purposes or the results are invalid. The general suggestibility of the subject in various motor tasks (i.e. body sway, etc.) would perhaps be an important variable to consider when investigating the extent to which a subject followed experimental directions versus his own personal inclinations in various tasks evaluating these personal equations (6).

Tests involving accurate movement could be investigated and correlations between scores elicited and various kinds of personal equations might be carried out. The relationship between selected personality traits (i.e. extroversion-introversion) and preferred extent and speed of movement might also prove interesting.

Overall, these investigations may provide a deeper understanding of some of the subtle nuances influential of perceptual-motor behavior. Correlation of these factors with various motor ability and motor learning tasks might explain some of the findings presently attributable to "experimental artifacts." Consideration of these kind of variables might also aid teachers and others working directly with children in schools to better understand the individual differences of their charges and encourage a more flexible approach by instructors attempting to elicit capacity measures from youths in various performance and classroom situations.

REFERENCES

1. Allport, G. W., and Vernon, P.E.: *Studies in Expressive Movements.* New York, Macmillan, 1933.
2. Bartley, Howard S.: *Principles of Perception.* New York, Harper, 1958.
3. Brengelmann, J. C.: Abnormal and personality correlates of certainty. *J Ment Sci, 105:*142, 1959.
4. Cratty, Bryant J., and Williams, H. G.: The accuracy of facing movements, executed without vision. Submitted for publication to *Res Quart,* March 1966.
5. Crutcher, R.: An experimental study of persistence. *J Appl Psychol, 18:*409, 1934.
6. Eysenck, H. J.: *The Structure of Human Personality.* London, Methuen, 1953.
7. Frischeisen-Kohler, L.: The personal tempo and its inheritance. *Character and Pers, 1:*301, 1933.
8. Harding, D. W.: Rhymization and speed of work. *Brit J Psychol, 23:*262, 1932.

9. Harrison, R., and Dovens, R. M.: Is rate of voluntary bodily movements unitary? *J Gen Psychol, 18:31, 1926.*
10. Kennedy, J. L., and Travis, R. C.: Prediction of speed of performance by muscle action potentials. *Science,* 105:410, 1947.
11. Lewis, F. H.: Affective characteristics of rhythm. *Psychol Bull, 30:679, 1933.*
12. MacArthur, R. S.: An experimental investigation of persistence and its measurement   at the secondary school level (unpublished Ph.D. Thesis). University of London Library, 1951.
13. Rethlingshafer, D.,: Relationship of tests of persistence to other measures of continuance of activities. *J Abnorm Soc Psychol, 37:71, 1942.*
14. Rimoldi, H.J.A.: Personal tempo. *J Abnorm Soc Psychol, 46:283,* 1951.
15. Ryans, D.G.: An experimental attempt to analyse persistence behavior: Measuring traits presumed to involve persistence. *J Gen Psychol, 19:333, 1938.*
16. Thornton, G. R.: A factor analysis of tests designed to measure persistence. *Psychol Monogr, 51:1,* 1939.

Chapter 12

WHY JOHNNY CAN'T RIGHT . . . WRITE . . .

ONE OF THE MORE vexing problems confronting teachers and parents is the determination of which hand the children in their charge should use when attempting to express their intellect on paper. It is not unusual to find children of seven years and older who seem confused when selecting a hand to engage in various one-handed classroom tasks. Children classified as retarded or neurologically handicapped frequently evidence confusion concerning hand usage well into adolescence.

The teacher is often introduced to psychological theories which suggest that the establishment of dominance is critical to the development of the intellect, and at the same time is confronted with children who, during a single writing lesson, may transfer their pencils from one hand to the other (10).

Fortunately there is experimental evidence which provides us a reasonably clear picture of the development of hand usage, as well as outlining practical methods for assessing hand preference of the immature or of the perceptually handicapped child. On the pages which follow, it will be attempted to present a brief survey of the research dealing with hand dominance; its etiology, relationship to other functions, and implications for the total educational process. The discussion will conclude with a practical method of assessing hand preference in children.

A search for an understanding of the genesis of hand preference in humans leads to literature in anthropology, child development, comparative anatomy, psychology, theology, and neurology. For example, in man's immediate ancestors, unilateral behavior was first seen about three million years ago in the australopithecine, who apparently wielded his club in his right hand judging from the holes in the left side of the baboon skulls found in the debris next to his weapons (9). This 85-pound, 4 feet six inch subhuman appears to be one of the earliest known toolmakers, although he boasted of a brain of only about one-third the size of that of modern man. Consulting the Bible, one comes upon evidence of the overriding predominance of right-handed functioning in humans, as it is mentioned that only about 700 out of 26,000 men in the tribe of Benjamin were left-handed or ambidextrous (Judges 20:15-16).

There are a number of studies attesting to the fact that upper-limb dominance, as reflected in preference of use, is seen in animals as low on the phylogenic scale as the rat. Peterson, in 1934, found that rats evidenced preference for either the right or left paw in equal numbers (24), while in a later study this same researcher studied the effects of attempting to retrain paw use and came to the conclusion that practice had only temporary effects upon this aspect of their behavior (25). Experimenters studying parrots, chimpanzees and cats have also found that hand or paw preference is experimentally discernible, rather well-fixed, and equally divided between the left and right "handers" (7,12). Finch, for example, found that only a minority of the chimpanzees he studied were ambidextrous. Cole concluded that this kind of unilateral behavior in cats might be traced to the variation in the number of fibers crossing to form the pyramidal tract in the spinal cord, rather than being caused by environmental influences.

Hand preference is seen rather early in the development of the human infant. While children cannot usually identify their left and right hands verbally when asked to do so until about the age of six or seven (15), they begin to exhibit the tendency to favor the use of one hand over the other as early as the fortieth week, and hand usage is relatively well-fixed by the first year. Most workers agree that no preference is seen prior to the seventh month of age. Orton and others have suggested that hand preference may tend to become unstable about the time the child learns to walk, only to reappear about a year later (21).

Gesell and others have suggested that left- or right-sidedness represents a kind of dynamic asymmetry first descernible as one observes the tonic-neck reflex in the infant. This reflex is not abolished but is submerged in bilateral patterns at about twenty-four weeks of age which are in turn subordinated to voluntary unilateral movement patterns after another month passes (15, p. 11-13).

As the growing child begins to exhibit more complex differentiated functions, his hand usage usually becomes well-fixed (22). By the age of seven all but about 15 percent of both boys and girls can correctly identify their left and right hands when they are pointed to, and hand use is usually well established (15). By the age of eight and nine years children are able to identify correctly the left and right hands of another person when asked to do so. It is thus apparent that hand usage precedes the ability to identify the left and right hand correctly by several years, while the ability to differentiate correctly the hands of another individual usually is seen after still another year passes.

When a child is able to make a correct identification of his left and right hands at six or seven years of age it is usually due to his ability to attach them to some function (18). For example, he may say that he uses his right hand to write, uses it for a pledge of allegiance, uses it to eat with, or some similar one-handed activity (18). Thus it seems that well-established hand use may hasten the later ability to cognitively identify the hands and their differences.

If, as proponents of Kephart's theory suggest, accurate left-right identification influences accurate judgements relative to direction in space, it would seem important to establish hand use early which will then elicit correct perceptions of the two sides of the body and their names. Wapner, however, studying the influence of asymetrical bodily tensions, experimentally induced, concluded that by late childhood the child begins to make spatial judgements relatively independent of his body (30).

Several other important questions have been dealt with by various experimenters throughout the years. For example, it appears from numerous investigations that hand usage when evaluated carefully leads one to the conclusion that there are degrees of right- or left-handedness. Several rating scales which will be discussed later reveal that individuals may be scored upon a continuum relative to the degree of hand preference they exhibit. (19,29,26).

Similarly tests of dominant ear, leg, and eye are often not predictive of hand usage. Individuals who are left-eye dominant, for example, are far more prevalent than are those who are left-handed (15). About 40 percent of the population are left-eyed, while only from 7 to 15 percent of various populations studied have been found to be left-handed. The incidence of mixed-dominance which these statistics suggest has been cause for concern among clinicians throughout the years; however, recent data by Ayres and others suggest that the "problem" may not be worthy of serious consideration. In the study cited it was found that mixed dominance was as prevalent in a population of normal children as it was in a population of children classified as neurologically handicapped (1).

Thus, dominance must be considered in the plural. There are a number of ways in which "mans" action system functions in asymetrical ways; functions which are at times independent of one another. For example, in a series of investigations of the veering tendency of the blind, we have found that the tendency to veer and to spiral when attempting to walk straight while consistent in direction is independent of arm or leg use, or of leg length (8)!

The etiology of hand usage has been the subject of experimental attention throughout the years. There is persuasive evidence that hand dominance is inherited. Data collected by Chamberlain, for example, lends support to this argument as it was found that the incidence of left-handed children with right-handed parents average about 2 percent; in families with one left-handed parent, left-handed children are found about 17 percent of the time; while if both parents throw from the port side they are likely to produce children with left-handed dominance about 46 percent of the time. It is likely, however, that both environmental factors and inherited factors summate to determine hand usage (4,5).

Similar to the studies cited previously with rats, it is usually found that children who evidence no marked tendencies to use either hand are more easily trained to the one or the other and tend less to retain a consistent hand usage as they grow up (24,28).

Getman and others have suggested as part of perceptual-motor training programs for children, practice in simultaneous bilateral hand movements (13). Generally, this practice involves drawing two circles and other geometric figures or conformations, one with either hand. It is difficult to find experimental evidence which supports the use of these kinds of coordination games. Although such exercises are difficult, and their performance improves with practice, this kind of bilateral activity would seem to interfere with establishing proficiency in the preferred hand. As has been noted, hand preference emerges rather early in the infant's development; to later encourage practice in various bilateral exercises of this nature seems unsound upon consideration of the available data.

Theories which propose that encouraging unilateral hand use will result in the remediation of a number of other functions conflicts with contemporary knowledge concerning hemispheric specialization. For if motorically, the left hemisphere regulates the use of the right hand, other functions seem distributed between both hemispheres. Although several years ago left hemispheric dominance was extended to all symbolic functions, within the last twenty years it has become recognized that lesions of the right hemisphere result in disorders of body image and spatial information. Left-sided representation for language is no longer disputed in the right-handed, however, the related problem of musical language is still open, and motor amusia may depend upon lesions of either hemisphere. Ideational apraxis and ideomotor apraxis depend exclusively upon left-sided lesions; visual-spatial disorders arise from right-sided lesions, while disorders more conceptual in nature are related to left-sided lesions. Digital agnosia (lack of awareness of fingers) is due to left-sided lesions. The acalculia (inability to calculate numbers) cannot be considered as an entity, but must be considered in parts. Inability to deal with figures and numbers cognitively is caused by left-sided lesions, whereas the ability to deal with numerical concepts spatially is disrupted by lesions in the right cerebral hemisphere (15,16).

These kinds of relationships could be extended and are presented to indicate how complex cerebral functioning is. The relationship between these functions and hand use is extremely remote. To suggest that somehow encouraging one-handed functioning will train other cognitive behaviors, one would not only have to assume some kind of intrahemispheric influence of one function (motor) upon another (perceptual-conceptual) which does not seem possible, but one would also have to assume some kind of cross-hemispheric influence which is even more remote from the contemporary findings of the neurologist.

Even though Eberhard recently found that simply watching the one-handed behavior of another individual while performing a manual skill will teach another subject the task as well as if the latter had performed it with his other hand first (11), most summaries of the problem of hand-usage, cerebral dominance, and similar topics conclude with the assertion that the early development of hand use is helpful (15). A child who decides upon his preferred hand at the age of five is able to practice more effectively for a longer time with that hand than a child who remains undecided for two or more years longer. It is therefore obvious that teachers and parents should make every effort to find out what tendencies a child exhibits and then encourage his use of that hand. Society usually demands that a child begin to perform in visual-manual skills about the age of five; if the child has not decided upon his preferred hand in an obvious way by that age, every effort should be made to assess his preference and to encourage him to utilize the hand he seems to prefer.

Assessment of hand preference by way of one-handed strength tasks, or even tasks of accuracy are not usually reliable. For frequently an individual will perform more accurately with his non-preferred hand or exert more pressure on a hand dynometer with his least-used hand. At the same time anatomical differences between preferred and non-preferred hand are also not reliable indices of hand use, nor are tests of tactile sensitivity (14).

While the use of the EEG and of various biochemical agents have been used with varying success to ascertain cerebral dominance, the methods open to the classroom teacher are less sophisticated (15,29). There are two general approaches to the assessment of hand preference: (a) performance tests in which the child is asked to execute various daily activities, and (b) questionnaires in which an observing parent is asked to specify the hand usage of their child (15).

The more complex the task required, the more likely the child will utilize his preferred hand. At the same time it is apparent that given seven or eight tasks, all so-called left-handers will not perform all seven with their left hand; at the same time right-handers will all not exhibit consistent unilateral behavior in their performances. Hecaen and others have reviewed these various techniques, ánd so an extensive review of them will not be attempted here (15).

The teacher might require the following seven tasks of a child and note the extent to which he performs each with a given hand. The performance of these should be required three times, on three different days, in order to obtain a valid measure of hand preference.

1. Throw a small ball at a target placed a reasonable distance away and of a size which will elicit success.
2. Place marbles in a bottle one by one. The neck of the bottle should be reasonably small.
3. Draw a square.
4. Thread a needle.

5. Comb the hair.
6. Place cards one by one into a small box which just barely contains them.
7. Cut out a circle with scissors.

In summary, it is suggested that hand preference appears in normal infants at a relatively early age, and at various times during their early development, it comes and goes. Awareness of the names of the hands on the part of the child is not evidenced until about the age of six and seven and is usually associated by the child with unilateral functioning.

Preferred hand usage has been documented in animals as primitive as rats, in subhumans living three million years ago, and in modern man living two thousand years ago. Hand usage is probably dependent upon inherited neuro-anatomical factors and is molded at times by environmental supports.

Promoting unilateral hand use to promote some kinds of improvement in central nervous system processes connected with various cognitive functions seems spurious upon consideration of available experimental evidence. At the same time, unilateral behavior as evidenced by the adoption of a preferred hand, by five years of age will permit more time in which to practice certain of life's necessary skills than is possible if this selection is delayed for several years.

With this in mind, the teacher should make an effort to assess hand preference in her charges and to encourage the child to make a consistent effort with the preferred hand following such an assessment.

REFERENCES

1. Ayres, Jean: Patterns of perceptual-motor dysfunction in children: A factor analytic study (Monogr Suppl.). *Percept Motor Skills 1-V20:*335, 1965.
2. Bingley, T.: Mental symptons in temporal lobe epilepsy and temporal lobe gliomas. *Acta Psychiat Neurol Scandinav,* 33(120):151, 1958.
3. Cernacek, J.: Contralateral motor irridation. Cerebral dominance. *Arch Neurol,* 4:165, 1961.

4. Chamberlain, H. D.: A study of some factors entering into the determination of handedness. *Child Develop, 6:*91, 1935.
5. Chamberlain, H. D.: The inheritance of left-handedness. *J Hered, 19:*557, 1928.
6. Clark, M. M.: *Left-handedness.* London, U. of London, 1957.
7. Cole, J.: Paw preference in cats related to hand preference in animals and man. *J Comp Physiol, 48:*137, 1955.
8. Cratty, Bryant J., and Williams, Harriet G: Perceptual Thresholds of Non-Visual Locomotion (Monogr). University of California, Los Angeles, 1966.
9. Dart, R.: *Adventures with the Missing Link.* New York, Harper, 1959.
10. Delacato, Carl H.: *The Diagnosis and Treatment of Speech and Reading Problems.* Springfield, Thomas, 1963.
11. Eberhard, Ulrich: Transfer of training related to finger dexterity. *Percept Motor Skills, 17:*274, 1963.
12. Finch, G.: Chimpanzee handedness. *Science, 94:*117, 1941.
13. Getman, Gerald: *Physiological Readiness.* Minneapolis, PASS, 1966.
14. Ghent, Lila: Developmental changes in factual thresholds on dominant and nondominant sides. *J Comp Physiol Psychol, 54:*670, 1961.
15. Hécaen, Henry, and de Ajuriaguerra, Julian: *Left-Handedness: Manual Superiority and Cerebral Dominance.* New York and London, Grune, 1964.
16. Hécaen, H., and Angelergues, R.: Etude anatomo-clinique de 280 cas de lésions reto-rolandiques unilatérales des hémisphères cérébraux. *Encephale, 6:*533, 1961.
17. Hertz, R.: La prééminence de la main droite. Étude sur la polarité religieuse. *Mélanges de Sociologie Religiuse et Folklore.* Paris, Alcan,
18. Ilg, Frances L., and Ames, Louise Bates: *School Readiness.* New York, Harper, 1965.
19. Jasper, H. H., and Raney, E. T.: The phi-test of lateral dominance. *Amer J Psychol, 49:*450, 1937.
20. Kephart, Newell C.: *The Slower Learner in the Classroom.* Columbus, Ohio, C. E. Merrill, 1956.
21. Orton, S.T.: Some studies in the language function. *Res Publ Ass Res Nerv Ment Dis, 13:*614, 1934.
22. Palmer, Robert D.: Development of a differentiated handedness. *Psychol Bull, 62:*257, 1964.
23. Palmer, Robert D.: Hand differentiation and psychological functioning, *J Personality, 31:*446, 1963.
24. Peterson, G. M.: Mechanisms of handedness in the rat. *Comp Psychol Monogr, 9:*1, 1934.
25. Peterson, G. M.: Transfer in handedness in the rat from forced practice. *J Comp Physiol Psychol, 44:*184, 1951.

26. Roudinesco, Mme, and Thyss, J.: L'enfant gaucher. Étude clinique. Signification physiologique. Problemès pédagogiques. *Enfance, 1:*8, 126, 1948.

27. Subirana, A.: La droiterie. *Arch Suisses Neurol Psychiat, 69:*1, 1952.

28. Tsai, L., and Maurer, S.: Right handedness in white rats. *Science, 74:*436, 1930.

29. Waada, J., and Rasmussen, T.: Intracaroit injection of sodium amytal for the lateralization of cerebral speech dominance. *J Neurosurg, 17:*266, 1960.

30. Wapner, Seymour, and Werner, Heinz: *Perceptual Development, An Investigation Within the Framework of Sensory-Tonic Field Theory.* Clark U. Press, 1957.

31. Wile, I. S.: *Handedness, Right and Left.* Boston, Lothrop, 1934.

32. Zangwill, O. L.: *Cerebral Dominance and Its Relation to Psychological Function.* London, Oliver and Boyd, 1960, Vol. I.

33. Zazzo, R.: *Les Jumeaux, le Couple et la Personne.* Paris, Presses Universitaires de France, 1960.

SECTION II

SPECIAL EDUCATION

A. General Considerations

Chapter 13

KINESIOLOGY AND SPECIAL EDUCATION

DURING THE PAST several years I have been engaged in two projects which I believe illustrate the very
direct way in which knowledge about man in action may
contribute to better living. One of these projects has been
a series of investigations dealing with the perceptual
judgments necessary as the blind move about their environment; the second is a clinical program for the improvement of children with mild perceptual-motor disturbances.

"PERCEPTUAL PERIPATOLOGY!"

The investigations with the blind arose from studies
which were intended to provide basic information about
motor learning. As with most researchers in learning, I
found it necessary to devise unique tasks with which the
subjects had had no prior experience and tasks which at
the same time evaluated the components of behavior in
which I was interested; the accuracy and speed with which
individuals can move. During a four year period extending
from 1961 to 1965, I constructed a series of large mazes
whose patterns were formed by plastic tubing placed waist
high and through which the blindfolded, sighted subjects
guided themselves using the backs of their hands or small
sticks held in their hands.

A speech presented to the Kinesiology Council of the American Association of Health,
Recreation and Physical Education at the National Convention in Chicago, Illinois,
March 21, 1966.

One is often asked how one obtains ideas for original research projects. I believe that about three avenues lie before the researcher. Initially and during the conduction of research, one must extend ones knowledge by drawing on other researchers' experiences. In short, he must devour the literature in large portions. Secondly, when working with human subjects, he must make note of every subtle nuance with which he is confronted. He must listen carefully when they wish to talk about the task he has presented them, and at times he must draw information from them by such general questions as "How do you feel?" "What did you think about that?" and the like. The third avenue to creative research is to spend a lot of time thinking, and during this time attempt to perceive relationships between two variables which have hither to not been examined as possibly related. It is this last avenue, I believe, which is the kernel of the creative process.

While listening to the subjects following their traversals of mazes, it became apparent that the experience they had undergone and the task which I had meant to present to them were at times two different things. Some curves in their patterns did not appear in the subjects' drawings executed immediately after traversal. At other times the subjects reported curves which were not present, while at still other times the subjects reported that we were omitting turns or were adding turns, when in truth the maze pattern had not been changed.

Noting these strange reactions we reprobed the literature and discovered the area of figural aftereffects in movement and in vision which could possibly explain some of the strange reports emanating from our subjects. Following this, pathways were constructed in the shape of half-circles, and various investigations in figural aftereffects elicited by the action of walking without vision were carried out. Distortions in the shape of these pathways were noted; for example, after walking pathways curved to the right, straight pathways were reported as seeming to curve left; similar distortions were produced when walking treadmills.

Again the reports of our subjects engaged in these

tasks were reexamined. Pathways which were obviously curved when visually inspected, were not reported curved by the blindfolded subjects when walking through them! It was found that we had to exceed some threshold to the perception of curvature in order to elicit the expected report and satiate a subject in the experience of right or left turning when walking without vision.

These latest disclosures led us to consult those people who might be expected to know something about the perception of the shape of a pathway walked without vision; the blind, and the people attempting to tutor them in accurate mobility. And it was here that we saw the need for research. Mobility trainers seemed to have only a superficial idea about what to expect in the way of perceptual judgments from their blind clients. Communication between the blind trainees in such programs and their instructors at times seemed to suffer from the fact that the reference systems from which each judged their environment were dissimilar. Thus due to encouragement from the blind and from mobility trainers, we have undertaken to collect basic data during the past two and one-half years concerning some of the variables influencing perceptual judgments formulated without the use of vision.

1. Using a large athletic field we found that the blind, like the sighted, veer, indeed spiral at the rate of about 40 degrees per 100 feet as they attempt to walk a straight line. Individuals who have been blind from birth or have been blind for a long period of time, however, seem to have learned their way out of this natural veering tendency.

2. The blind seem to be more accurate in their judgment of gradient while walking over it than are the sighted when inspecting the same surface with vision. Many of the blind reported 1 degree of decline, while we had to measure these same risers in order to determine whether they were truly slanted or not.

3. Humans are more sensitive to decline than to incline when walking without vision.

4. The threshold for the sensitivity to path curvature

when walking without vision is one with a radius of about forty-five to fifty feet.

5. People tend to overturn facing movements of about 90 degrees made without vision but characteristically underturn facing movements of 180 and 360 degrees.

6. Other data is being collected and analyzed this year, including on the sensitivity to left-right tilt in pathways walked, the trainability of the veering tendency, the sensitivity to the curvature of curbs (using a cane to determine curvature), ability to reposition the body, and the relations of these perceptual judgments to measures of emotional stability, anxiety, and intelligence. The veering tendency of the arms when attempting to draw straight versus total body veer is being explored. The repositioning ability of the arms versus the total body is also undergoing investigation.

Following the first year's work an orientation test for the blind was constructed in order to evaluate individual differences in the perception of gradient, veering tendency, etc. It is intended to add to the items in this battery following the second year's work. Thus norms are being collected from which to assess individual differences and to evaluate the success of various training techniques which might be applied (See Appendix).

One overriding finding which has implications for physical educators concerns the fact that the veering tendency is related not to structural but to perceptual factors. Leg length, posture, and similar structural qualities were predictive neither of the amount nor of the direction of veer. People, both blind and sighted, move their bodies; their bodies do not move them. The blind walk where they think they should go. People are not little wind-up toys to be turned off and on in physical endeavors. Man is not simply a series of levers and pulleys but an organism capable of volitional acts, influenced by his motives, molded by his values, sensitive to the situation, and capable of modifying his efforts by assessing his past experience. Failure to consider some of these concepts, I believe, makes us less capable as educators of the sighted children in our charge.

THE CLUMSY CHILD SYNDROME

For the past four years I have also conducted a program for children who have been identified by pediatricians, child psychologists, child psychiatrists and educators as evidencing mild perceptual-motor problems. We have worked with from twenty to fifty children per week, and at the present time have the program within the confines of the University. Although such children evidence a wide variety of behavior, two types of children will be discussed briefly: (a) the hyperactive child, and (b) the boy with problems of gender identification.

The hyperactive child has been identified in a number of ways; as lacking impulse control, being "ground-oriented," and/or as distractible. Generally he is unable to attend to any task for any length of time. He evidences perceptual problems involving figure-ground relationships, "motor disinhibition," and lacks the ability to synthesize parts of his environment into wholes.

Essentially, the job of the kinesiologist is to provide motor activities which focus him for a period of time longer than he has perhaps ever attended to anything before. Taking a lead from educators experienced with working with such children, we attempt to provide an environment which is distraction-free and contains learning experiences which are in themselves stimulating and attention-getting. The problem thus seems to encourage relative immobility with motor activities, perhaps a blasphemous thought to a group of physical educators.

Following several years work with these children, attempts to invoke the "drainage" theory do not seem helpful. To attempt to dissipate these excess energies seems about as promising as attempting to lower the interest in sex by showing people sexy pictures. Recent work by Lovass and others also suggests that using motoric activities to drain excess hostility will meet with similar failure.

It has been found that selected types of motor activities (i.e. balance-beam walking) can serve to lengthen the attention span of these children. At the same time, it has been difficult to measure comparable improvement in classroom attention span, although the potential for research in this area is apparent.

GENDER IDENTIFICATION

Gender identification on the part of children occurs rather early and at times is different from their biological sex. Some authorities suggest that gender is the result of early human imprinting similar to the type of learning which occurs as certain perceptual events are encountered early in the life of animals.

The child with problems in this area at an early age adopts gesture patterns and games of the opposite sex, prefers to dress in inappropriate clothes, and at times voices the wish to become a member of the opposite sex.

In general, the reasons for the atypical behavior range from the biological to the social. However, in general, the family unit in which this problem is found in the case of boys includes a dominant mother, older sisters, and a father who is ineffectual or absent. The male with this problem early in life incurs the displeasure of his male peers. He bothers them, although at first they cannot quite say why.

A leading expert in the area of male homosexuality recently told me that about 70 per cent of the male deviates whom she has interviewed during the past years informed her that their first confrontation with male games were traumatic experiences; that they had actively sought help in the assumption of appropriate skills at this time, and when rejected, reverted to solitary activities or to companionship of others who had been similarly rejected.

The problem is a complex one. We have found in our program that we can quickly change the observable movements of the children with whom we work; the extent to which this exerts some permanent change is debatable. Their movements, however, are the primary means by which their peers judge them and a major cause for parental concern.

Educators sensitive to this problem need to approach

its solution from several standpoints. Initially, rather specific instruction should probably be offered to these children in sex-appropriate activities, vigorous skills in the case of boys and perhaps dance activities for the girls. At the same time the instructors in such a program should become sensitive to the subtle "pick-up" of gestures by children and should at all times present an appropriate image to their charges.

SUMMARY

Through the years, innumerable other areas of research and service related to education have become apparent. One only has to dispel the channelized thinking which is evidenced in statements which begin "Physical educators are not interested in...." In lieu of this, we should have acquired enough self-confidence to say that "As researchers whose primary focus is upon man in action we stand ready to...."

The area of early childhood education vitally needs our insights and research skills. Children whose perceptual-motor problems are not pronounced enough to consign them to special schools, yet whose incapacities make them the "worst kid in the class," seek our help. The blind can benefit from the knowledge we possess and may discover about kinesthesis, while the neurologically impaired can be aided by drawing on our store of information about the teaching of motor skills.

Our function in education can continue to be an important one. At the clinical level we can help people; as researchers we can help people help people. The opportunities for service are pressing, while the opportunities for research seem limitless.

Chapter 14

ON THE THRESHOLD

IN THE NOT TOO distant past, arriving at the truth was a relatively simple matter. One had only to listen to and to obey the voice of authority. Adhering to the pronouncements of the clergy and the commands of the reigning monarch took much of the hazard out of making individual judgments.

Today the world is more complex. Rational men test their beliefs by reference to the scientific method of problem solving. This newer avenue to the truth results in greater accuracy. Observations are confirmed or disproved through analyses of measurable evidence, employing techniques which others can understand and may replicate.

But this approach to the truth has also produced special problems. Examples are the debates in the medical literature concerning the influence of smoking upon lung cancer, the use of oral contraceptives, and the value of certain drugs in the treatment of psychotic disturbances. Similar disagreements are currently aired in educational journals. These controversies are brought about by the failure to agree upon two fundamental problems: (a) the type of evidence which is considered to be scientifically valid, and (b) the way in which research findings should be interpreted.

But controversy is healthy. Arguments refine the issues. Questions hone the edges of reason and should

The 1965 Merck, Sharpe and Dohm Lecture, sponsored by the Texas Institute of Child Psychiatry, Baylor University Medical Center, Houston, Texas, December, 1965.

eventually lead men to an even greater capacity to understand their environment and themselves.

Physical educators have not been immune to controversy. In the 1930's, it was declared by some that we were the salvation of America's educational system. Overreacting to the preachments of Dewey and Kilpatrick, certain writers asserted that we were working with the whole individual through physical activities and in this manner, contributed directly to his social adjustment. We became psychiatrists in the ball field!

However, objective evidence supporting this philosophical stand was tenuous to say the least. For example, one investigator concluded that sports participation aided social adjustment because college girls in physical education classes were able to name more of their classmates at the end of the semester than at the beginning! Participation in physical activity was the cause advanced for increased sociality, although no causal relationship had been proved. The hyperactive physical social "lion" was revered; the happy, productive introvert was abhorred despite some evidence that social hyperactivity may be reflective of neurotic behavior. The playfield does provide a dynamic workshop for social interaction, but so does the bridge game.

Other research indicated that boys scoring higher on personal adjustment scales had stronger grip strength scores (13) - The implication? Of course, strengthen the grip and improve personal adjustment!! It was assumed that because A was related to B, it must *cause* B. However, the logician would cry *post hoc, ergo propter hoc,* while the statistician would mutter that correlation is not causation (18).

In 1956 Sputnik circled the world; shifts in educational goals occurred from an emphasis upon producing an adjusted child to the development of curricula designed to fashion the productive child. Scientific-mindedness replaced "well-roundness"; math-science scholarships usurped athletic grants-in-aid as status symbols. Child-rearing literature began to contain articles concerned with achievement needs, reading at two, and the role of the home in improving the child's learning capabilities.

Physical educators have not been slow to react. Spurred on by the theoretical pronouncements of a psychologist in the Midwest, a school seating engineer in Florida, and a doctor of education in Philadelphia, it has been suggested that motor activities contribute to an even wider variety of human capabilities than was dreamed about in the 1930's (16,14,10,3). Crawling improved hearing, speaking, thinking, seeing, perceiving, and cognition. Walking a balance board aids reading by heightening laterality. *Physiological optics, neurological organization,* and *laterality-directionality* supplemented bland educational terms. The trampoline was raised in status from the prop of a carnival clown to the indispensable diagostic tool of the clinical neurologist. The nervous system was reduced to four simple components that everyone could understand. Instead of handing their teacher an apple upon entering school each morning, children began the day by creeping around her desk.

Rousseau's *recapitulation theory* appeared in a new suit (17). Rousseau suggested that the child passes through five successive stages: the animal stage from birth to five; the savage stage from five to twelve years of age; early adolescence signals the start of the pastoral stage when reason and judgment are beginning to awaken in the youth; followed by the social stage; finally culminating in the adult stage which ends in a marriage to the ideal girl. This type of recapitulation theory, initiated by Rousseau in the late eighteenth century, was echoed for the next two-hundred years and appeared in various forms in literature dealing with anthropology, philosophy, education, and even in neurology. Typical in the neurology texts of the middle nineteenth century were references to a type of *lamination* theory which suggested that the nervous system of the child develops in discrete layers from structures mediating relatively simple functions to the more complex neurological functions carried on by the cerebral cortex.

But these new theories have bred healthy controversy, and, I believe, raised several questions which demand answers: (a) Does one merely have the obligation to outline techniques for perceptual-motor training without providing a scientifically sound theory underlying these techniques? Is it important to know *why* you are doing something which *seems* to improve learning in the classroom? (b) What is the status of knowledge about the human nervous system, about learning, about motor activity, and about the interaction between classroom learning and movement activities? (c) What kinds of perceptual-motor training programs may enhance learning and which activities seem superfluous?

Elucidation of these questions is important, because it seems to me that the parent and school district which quickly adopt new and controversial practices, i.e. crawling ten minutes a day, will be the same individuals and groups who, when subsequently failing to find the expected gains in measures of classroom learning success, will also be the first to relegate perceptual-motor activities back to the underfinanced, understaffed, and "sweaty" position they previously held. And this I believe would be extremely unfortunate.

Let us examine for a few moments, then, the scientific validity of the practices and most important the tenability of the theories espoused by Kephart, Delacato, and Harmon. This evaluation will be followed by some recommendations for positive action.

Basic to the correct application of the scientific method to the study of behavioral change is a determination of the influence of one variable at a time upon the performance measure under consideration. For if lots of things happen to people in a program of perceptual-motor training, it is important to determine which of these really help, which are of no assistance, and which ones perhaps work against the hoped-for objectives.

Thus, of paramount importance is the enumeration of some of the variables which perhaps could influence relationships between A (crawling) and B (a reading improvement score). For example, if we ask, or require, that a child crawl for thirty minutes (assuming that we do not ask him to do anything else), there are at least six accompanying factors which could change scores recorded on succeeding tasks: (a) His attention span might be lengthened, because the child has engaged in an activity longer than he usually attends to anything; (b) Personal rapport has been established between an instructor and his charge. An adult has been attentive to the child for a period of time; (c) Vigorous motor activity has reduced biochemical indices of stress in the blood. Muscular tension decreases following exercise. The child becomes more relaxed; (d) Vigorous movements of the legs promote a heightened awareness of their location. They become stronger and begin to move more effectively in other tasks; (e) A "success syndrome" has been established, the child has perhaps accomplished something, while perhaps in the past he has performed poorly at nearly everything; (f) Arising from these programs are positive and clear-cut formulas for improvement which undoubtedly aid in reducing parent-child tensions which are usually present, particularly when the child has a mild or severe perceptual-motor difficulty. The child perceives the parent acting positively as opposed to rejecting or overprotecting him. A constructive course of action is apparently being taken to help improve his problem of which he is many times acutely aware.

But of equal importance is the examination of the theoretical underpinnings of some of these movement programs. The Philadelphian's theory is widely published and discussed (3). It is easy to understand because it is simple. Ontogeny parallels phylogeny; train the central nervous system rather than educate peripheral functions, neurologically "organize" the child by recapitulating his total development through practice of the gross movements which characterize various developmental stages.

From birth to sixteen weeks of age, the infant primarily engages in reflex writhings resembling movements of the fish, and these are mediated by the spinal cord and medulla oblongata, according to Delacato. At the next higher level, reached at about sixteen weeks, the actions of the infant are mediated by the pons, and the movements primarily characteristic of this stage involve homolateral crawling supported by the tonic neck reflex, also seen in the locomotor patterns of amphibians. At about the sixth month of age the infant begins to move into the mid-brain stage of development characterized by creeping, moving in a cross-extension pattern, with the mid-brain as the prime level structure involved. A third dimension is added to the child's movements as he begins to leave the floor and assume an upright posture. He then resembles a mammal in his movements.

The next step in the progression toward complete human functioning is the development of cortical hemispheric dominance usually evidenced by hand choice; purportedly a trait unique in man. This final stage takes place between five to eight years of age, it is advanced.

Delacato further suggests that if a child has problems in reading, hearing or seeing, or other perceptual difficulties, one should attempt to train the motor behavior which is controlled by the neural structures which also mediate the sensory-motor deficiencies noted in the child. Thus, a parent in Los Angeles, for example, was recently asked to pattern her child's sleep every two hours in the characteristic tonic-neck position; creeping for an hour a day is also a frequent prescription. It is also suggested by Delacato that a child be removed from all tonal experience, as according to Delacato, tonality is mediated by the non-dominant half of the cerebral hemisphere. In addition emphasis is placed upon creeping as it is supposed to enhance cortical functioning, important to effective speaking, hearing, visual perception, and learning of normal children.

Five major deficiencies can be identified in this theoretical construct:

1. The functioning of the nervous system is not as simple as it is assumed to be by this theory. Voluntary motor patterns are the product of dynamic interactions of innumerable areas of the brain; some initiating, others suppressing, and others timing the actions. Evidence of the interrelated nature of structures within the central

nervous system is vividly portrayed when one studies findings concerning the functions of the reticular activating system, researched by Magoun and his co-workers at the University of California.

This mass of undifferentiated neurons extending from the top of the spinal cord through the brain stem up into the thalamus and hypothalamus, acts as a response selector and is connected to both motor and sensory pathways by branching fibers. Measurements made by means of fine electric probes placed within this system reveal that the responses of its neurons are largely "unspecific"; it thus appears to perform a kind of summation of the overall nervous activity of the organism.

There is direct evidence that this system interacts with muscles and glands, serving to awaken selected nervous circuits and to desensitize other circuits involving several structures of the central nervous system simultaneously.

The reticular activating system also serves to correct movements once initiated when additional sensory information is received during the performance of a complex task. This system is thus involved in the control of a wide range of muscular and glandular responses, providing the mechanisms for selecting responses from many different behavioral programs involving several portions of the brain and thus prevents what might otherwise be chaotic, uncontrolled competition among various modes of response. Evidence also indicates that the reticular activating system controls attention and even consciousness. The complex functioning of reticular activating system, chosen as an example here, points clearly to the *inter*dependence of the structures of the central nervous system.

While time does not permit us to explore further some of the other areas of recent research which refute Delacato's philosophical neurology, the investigations by Penfield on the neural control of speech, and of memory localization, and the split-brain studies by Sperry, further serve to make obsolete Delacato's nineteenth century neural lamination theory.

Although in earlier years the nervous system was compared to a telephone switchboard, and the function of the brain was likened to an operator handling calls coming in from sense organs; sorting them out and plugging each one into an outgoing line that connected it to the appropriate muscle or gland, today we know enough about the brain to reject such a superficial analogy, just as the oversimplified theory proposed by Delacato to explain neural development should also be rejected.

Creeping, for example, is the product of a neuromotor "program" initiated in the cerebrum, involving both the associative and motor areas. The reticular activating system contributes to the general tension level accompanying the movement, while the cerebellum "smooths" the act by involvement in certain of its timing components. The locomotor reflex, mediated at the spinal level, may underline the gross characteristics of the cross-extension pattern evidenced.

Confirmation of this principle of dynamic interaction has been so thoroughly established in experimental neurology that it has been codified as Hughling Jackson's principle, i.e. motor output is a finite resultant of the interactions of several portions of the nervous system. Experimental evidence supporting this principle is also obtained when a portion of the central nervous system is experimentally ablated or is damaged by accident or disease and then an attempt is made to assess the role of the structure damaged by observing motor output. The exact relationship between function and damage is rarely discernible, as it is usually difficult to determine whether the ablated area was a controlling mechanism, an inhibiting or a facilitating structure influencing the action pattern under consideration.

2. There is a scarcity of data supporting the assumption that motor activity of the large postural and limb muscles affects the visual or the associative centers of the brain. While irradiation occurs between neurons closely aligned, to hypothesize that a given set of nerve pathways somehow changes other nerve pathways structurally or functionally which pass through a proximal

portion of the central nervous system has little supportive evidence.

3. The data which are advanced in support of Delacato's theoretical suppositions have been gained by clinicians watching the gross behavior of children and then explaining the observations by hypothesizing neurological underpinnings. Physical educators and psychologists have engaged in this type of philosophical neurology for years. It should be recognized for what it is, no matter where it occurs or who utters it.

4. Delacato's theory is based to a large degree upon the importance of establishing laterality and thus improving complex symbolic behavior and abstract reasoning. Some of the supportive evidence cited relates to the finding that the australopithecine usually swung his bone club in his right hand when bashing out the brains of unfortunate baboons which he encountered (2). However, this 4 foot 6 inch, 85-pound apeman, while possessing a round, humanlike pelvis which enabled him to engaged in erect locomotion, could boast of a cranial capacity which was less than one-third that of most modern men (600 cc as compared to 1500-2200cc). Thus, Delacato postulates that a modern brain which was more than tripled in size has only to be "trained" by engaging in gross unilateral motor behavior that was characteristic of a subhuman living in South Africa about 2 million years ago!

5. Literature in child development provides a fifth source of information which is in conflict with Delacato's theories. Innumerable findings point to the superficiality of Delacato's observations with regard to the motor-mental development of children. Delacato suggests that the infant is "bound by his reflexes" when first born, although Preyer and others have found that the fetus evidences crude voluntary movements before birth. Delacato suggests that basic locomotor patterns proceed before the establishment of laterality, while Gierseke and others observe evidences of unilateral behavior based upon hand choice as early as seventeen weeks of age, well before the child has begun to creep. Gesell and the majority of child development experts state that children develop in a series

of spirals, moving ahead in several types of behavior at a time, sometimes retrogressing and latter "filling in" developmental skills rather than in the smooth, orderly sequence hypothesized by Delacato. Delacato seems unique in his observations concerning the characteristics of children's sleep patterns. All parents are aware of the multitude of positions that children fall into during a night's sleep. To suggest that a child who does not usually assume the tonic neck position may be headed for later problems is questionable. A child sleeping on his face *must* turn his head to one side to breathe. And due to the structural characteristics of the shoulder and hip region he *must* place his body in a position simulating a tonic neck position.

Others have advanced more palatable theoretical formulations which do not necessitate the assumption that the central nervous system is being trained by motor activities. Harmon and Kephart's theories are more peripheral in nature. They suggest that perceptual-motor training enhances classroom learning by adjusting and balancing postural tensions (10,11) and by heightening the child's perceptions of his body, particularly left-right discrimination (14). It is believed that these assumptions are supported by more valid evidence and are probably accepted by a reasonably large percentage of the professional workers in education, psychotherapy, psychiatry, psychology. The child development literature for the past thirty years supports the importance of sensory-motor experience in the early learning of children, while the importance of the body as the frame of reference from which perceptual judgments involving vision are formed has also been documented with some frequency in the experimental literature (8,9).

However, these theories also lack experimental evidence indicating *which* of the varied techniques suggested are actually affecting various perceptual attributes. Harmon, for example, published data which indicated that learning in the experimental classrooms in Winter Haven, Florida, showed only slight improvement over that evidenced in the "control" classrooms (11).

But what evidence *is* available which will shed some light upon the nature of motor activity and its relationship to classroom learning? The neurological journals, child development monographs, and experiments from the psychological laboratories for the past seventy-five years have fortunately contributed findings which *do* relate to these problem. areas. So let us enumerate some of these and from them derive some purposeful courses of action.

Finding

The motor attributes of children are highly specific and tend to become more so with age and experience. For example, there are at least three kinds of balances, four kinds of strengths, several kinds of attributes involving agility and power. For instance, balancing in a static position is unrelated to moving balance (i.e. walking a balance beam). Balance with the eyes open is unrelated to the same task attempted with the eyes closed, while the ability to balance objects is unrelated to the individual's ability to balance his body. Furthermore, static strength is unrelated to a ballistic strength necessary to jump or to throw a ball. Abdominal strength and grip strength are usually not related. Manual dexterity may be factored into at least five components (4,5,6,7).

Implication for Action. To properly evaluate and to improve the perceptual-motor ability of children one should provide a number of tasks involving balance, agility, hand-eye coordination, manual dexterity, strength, and flexibility, depending upon the deficiencies assessed.

Finding

Perceptual judgments and motor functioning are at times impossible to separate. For example, catching a ball involves the visual tracking of a moving object in three-dimensional space, perceptually anticipating its pathway while moving the body to intercept it, and then placing the hands in proper catching position.

Implication for Action. Perception probably is being trained while engaging in many movement experiences.

Handwriting, ball throwing, and tracking visually the words across a written page from left to right are not purely perceptual or motor acts but should be termed perceptual-motor tasks.

Finding

Muscular tension facilitates direct forceful acts while inhibiting complex coordinations.

Implication for Action. To improve complex perceptual-motor performances of children, place them in situations where social-emotional "tone" does not contribute to muscular tension if you expect them to learn complex skills.

Finding

Many times complex tasks can be learned by children with severe perceptual-motor problems if the skills are reduced to simple components and the child is reinforced, i.e. given reassurance from the instructor, etc., when even slight improvement is evidenced (12).

Implication for Action. When working with children with mild to severe problems, reduce the tasks to basic components; when these are mastered, proceed to build up more complex response patterns upon these beginnings.

Finding

The manner in which the child perceives his body, moves his body, and locates and uses his body parts is influential of some learnings during early childhood.

Implication for Action. Work with basic perceptual tasks prior to proceeding to more complex ones (i.e. reading). Find out if the child can locate his body relative to an object (i.e. stand in front of that box, put your left side toward the line, etc.); tumbling, trampolining, and other similar activities serve to heighten awareness of the large surfaces of the body. Require verbal feedback from the child as he identifies his hands, wrists, knees, etc. and engages in unilateral activities to heighten the ability to make different left-right judgments about his body. By constructing a solid "body platform," a base is provided from which accurate and more complex judgments may then be made.

Finding

More important than the performance level in a task is how the individual *feels* about his level of achievement. Success is measured not in absolutes but in comparison with real or hypothesized norms (1). If the individual perceives himself continually failing, an overlay of emotional-muscular tension results which further impedes learning.

Implication for Action. To heighten an individual's self-concept, provide situations in which he experiences success, even though slight. Success is related to the values of the individual performing. Thus, a boy between the ages of five and fifteen, whose peers highly regard prowess in sports can be expected to base a large portion of his self-concept upon his success or failure in physical activities. To heighten a youngster's self-concept, part of his educational program should be devoted to improving socially valued physical skills. There is evidence that a "failure syndrome" on the playground will begin to generalize to the classroom and that success in sports may also transfer to other behavior.

To perform with at least average ability is important to the self-concept of growing boys in our culture. If he cannot move well, compensatory behavior may take one or more of three forms: (a) He will retreat into intellectual endeavors—he becomes a Ph.D. at age ten, he leaves the play yard, and tensions mount; (b) He becomes a supercilious "court jester," making light of performance situations—he feels it is better to be noticed in this way than not noticed at all; he becomes giggly and feminine in his approach to problems involving overt activity; (c) perhaps the most serious of all, he totally rejects himself, characterized by a withdrawal from competition and performance in a variety of tasks both intellectual and physical.

Finding

Although extensive experimental evidence is still lacking, there are indications that gross movement at times provides a sensory experience which will enhance general classroom learning. For example, in my program we attempt to lengthen attention span by providing movement experiences which require successively longer periods of time to complete, i.e. lengthening a balance beam. If attention is taken away from the beam it becomes obvious to the observer and to the performer. Recently we have had a hyperactive boy whose attention span was initially clocked at eight seconds engage in an obstacle course which required from forty-five seconds to one minute of his attention. It is hoped that such improvement will transfer to the classroom.

Another attribute needed in classroom learning, specifically when reading and spelling, is the ability to order items in a correct series. To spell, one must correctly place letters in a series; and to recognize a phrase, a similar process must take place. With this in mind we have utilized obstacle courses of varying complexities and lengths in the the attempt to not only enhance the motor qualities necessary to negotiate its various components, but also to teach the child to correctly negotiate the sub-tasks in a given order. Whether this is done or not is clearly apparent to the observing teacher far more apparent than the flicking of an eye across a printed page.

Based upon experimental evidence obtained in our laboratory, it seems that the learning of letters and geometric shapes may be enhanced by placing large letters and shapes on a playground and devising games on them involving their traversal. For years our games have consisted of squares and circles; why not include triangles, hexagons, and letters of the alphabet on our elementary school playgrounds? Gross movement may thus provide another important type of sensory experience through which components of the learning process may be enhanced. Activities of the total body may serve to focus the hyperactive child's attention.

CONCLUSIONS

As you have been able to tell, I agree with some of the practices and theories which have been recently advanced and question others. We should, I believe, be critical but open-minded. Professional people visiting Philadelphia usually come away impressed; improvement does seem to take place in the behavior of children subjected to this program of motor training. But we should not overact. While some of these theories are difficult to defend experimentally, perhaps some component of these practices do indeed influence the nervous system in ways not fully understood at the present time.

In the late 1700's, Luigi Galvani, public lecturer in anatomy at the University of Bologna, stimulated the nerve endings of dead frogs with a Leyden jar, eliciting a muscular twitching that caused a great stir in the civilized world, as it was interpreted that he was restoring life to dead animals and perhaps could do the same for humans. Galvani, by beginning to explore the nature of nerve impulse transmission was making a significant contribution, while the overactions of the public came to naught.

Those of us in universities with research budgets and the time to carry out well-controlled studies need to persist in our efforts to substantiate or negate some of the theoretical assumptions advanced and the practices arising from them. And hopefully through these means, new and important dimensions will be reached in our service to children.

The movements people engage in *are* important. They comprise that component of overall behavior which others can see and react to. To a large degree the self-concept of the young is based upon what they can do with their bodies. And yet movement is not the key from which all the mental, emotional, and social facets of personality must necessarily stem (1). Perceptual-motor malfunctions of a mild or severe nature can be caused by lesions in the nervous system, by biochemical imbalances, and/or can be attributed to deep-seated emotional problems. There is little evidence that any of these can be influenced by crawling on the floor.

The key to helping a child with learning problems is to first understand the child. Improvement in behavior of people cannot be gained by inserting them into a formula. We should synthesize available knowledge, not ignore it. The answer to complexity is not a retreat to simplicity.

REFERENCES

1. Cratty, Bryant J.: *Movement Behavior and Motor Learning.* 2nd ed. Philadelphia, Lea and F., 1967.
2. Darwin, C. *Adventures with the Missing Link.* New York, Harper, 1959.
3. Delacato, Carl H.: *The Diagnosis and Treatment of Speech and Reading Problems.* Springfield, Thomas, 1964.
4. Fleishman, E.A.: The dimensions of physical fitness—the nation-wide normative and developmental study of basic tests. Technical Report No. 4, The Office of Naval Research, Department of Psychology, Yale University, August 1962.
5. Fleishman, E.A.: Factorial analysis of complex psychomotor performance and related skills. *J Appl Psycho, 40:2,* 1956.
6. Fleishman, E.A., and Ellison, Gaylor D.: A factor analysis of fine manipulative tests. *J Appl Psycho, 46:96,* 1962.
7. Fleishman, E.A.; Kremer, Elmar J., and Shoup, Guy W.: The dimensions of physical fitness—A factor analysis of strength tests. Technical Report No. 2, The Office of Naval Research, Department of Industrial Administration and Department of Psychology, Yale University, August 1961.
8. Frostig, Marianne, and Horne, David: *The Frostig Program for the Development of Visual Perception: Teacher's Guide.* Chicago, Follett, 1964.
9. Gesell, Arnold: *Vision.* New York, Hoeber, 1949.
10. Harmon, Darell B.: *Notes on a Dynamic Theory of Vision.* Published by author, 1958, Vol. I.
11. Harmon, Darell B.: *Winter-Haven Study of Perceptual Learning.* Winter-Haven Lions Research Foundation, Inc., Winter-Haven Lions Club, Winter-Haven, Florida, 1962.
12. Hirsch, William: *Motor skill transfer by trainable mentally retarded and normal children.* (Doctoral Dissertation). University of California at Los Angeles, 1962.
13. Jones, Harold E.: Physical ability as a factor in social adjustment in adolescence. *J Educ Res, 40:287,* 1946.
14. Kephart, Newell C.: *The Slower Learner in the Classroom.* Columbus, Ohio, C. E. Merrill, 1960/63.
15. Piaget, Jean: *The Construction of Reality in the Child.* New York, Basic Books, 1954.

16. Radler, and Kephart, N.C.: *Success Through Play*. New York, Harper, 1963.
17. Rousseau, J.J.: *Emile*, or *Education*, by B. Foxley. London, Dent, 1911.
18. Slater-Hammel, A.T.: Problem of evidence in research. Speech given to the International Federation of Sports Psychology, Rome, Italy, April 1965.
19. Stoltz, H.R., and Stoltz, L.M.: Adolescent problems related to somatic variations *Adolescence* (43rd Yearbook N.S.S.E., Part I). Chicago, U. of Chicago 1944.
20. Wapner, Seymour, and Werner, Heinz: *Perceptual Development, An Investigation Within the Framework of Sensory-Tonic Field Theory*. Clark U. Press, 1957.

Chapter 15

WE LEARN OF VISION FROM THE SIGHTLESS, AND THE RETARDED TEACH US ABOUT COGNITION

THERE IS FREQUENT concern expressed when some of us in physical education become interested in various problems of the atypical child. This interest is sometimes cited as additional evidence that we are truly moving farther away from the child on the playground. Sometimes this interest may be prompted by the fact that more funds are usually available to study the child with various problems than are available to research the motor skills of normal children. In any case more and more interest is being accorded by physical educators to children and youths with various kinds of subtle and obvious learning problems.

Within recent years my basic research in motor learning led me to the study of problems involving kinesthetic aftereffects (5). Distortions by subjects while traveling through large mazes, relative to the pathways' conformations, led us to attempt to design equipment specifically to create various kinds of perceptual illusions. While attempting to do this we began to explore various threshold measures which we believed might be known by individuals working with the blind. Knowledge about thresholds of the perception of curvature in pathways when walking gradients without vision was critical to our studies, but we found that no evidence of this type was available. This gap in the knowledge prompted our five-year program dealing with the blind, presently in its second year.

Speech given to the Conference on Motor Learning and Movement Education, Friday, February 3, 1967, sponsored by the Department of Physical Education, The University of Wisconsin, Milwaukee.

Six years ago we initiated a program for the improvement of neurologically handicapped children. During these years we have worked with from thirty-five to fifty children per week, and presently have twelve part-time employees in this program which encompasses training in manual skills, in gross movement activities, and in such practical skills as bicycle riding.

Last summer I was asked to a meeting of "interested individuals," and upon arriving found myself an "administrator" of a program designed to evaluate the perceptual-motor abilities of over two hundred retarded children within the Los Angeles area. This pilot study is being used as a basis for a county-wide program involving five hundred subjects which will continue for a two-year period and will be designed to evaluate the effects of perceptual-motor training upon various measures of emotional, social, intellectual, and motor development (4).

When carrying out these projects, vast amounts of data have been collected. For example, 283 retarded children were tested individually in about fifty tasks this summer. Research projects are presently underway with the neurologically handicapped children in our clinic program. Over 350 blind persons from four to eighty-six years of age have been evaluated for up to two days each in our research program with the blind.

But one might ask the question (and it is asked with some frequency by various of my colleagues) What good are you doing for the "normal" child?° It is believed that the following statements may answer this persistent question. As we analyzed the data and observed and questioned our subjects, it became increasingly apparent that the blind were not only aiding us to devise programs for their own education, but were also teaching us about the many ramifications of the role of vision in the performance and

---

°Locating a normal child is often difficult. Teachers in special education attending an institute given by the writer recently were asked to compare various perceptual-motor attributes of a retarded child with those of a normal child. Without exception the teachers were able to locate a retarded child, but experienced great difficulty finding a child truly free from some kind of emotional, social, motor, and/or cognitive defect.

learning of various perceptual-motor tasks by the sighted. The retarded were aiding us to develop sequences of perceptual-motor tasks for application to "normal" children. The neurologically handicapped youngster has also supplied us with data which have enabled us more exactly to structure sequential presentation of motor tasks which are applicable to the preschool child and to the child with only minor motor difficulties.

THE ROLE OF VISION IN MOVEMENT

For years many scholars interested in various phases of child development have referred to the importance of movement experiences to the perceptual and cognitive development of the child. Piaget, among others, has alluded to the critical impact of the "sensory motor period" within the developmental ladder.

However, one could make an even stronger case for the role of visual experience in the perceptual development and intellectual development of children. According to the studies of Dennis and others, restricting the movements of Indian children does nothing to impede their motor development (8). Similarly the data recently published by Abercrombie and her research staff from London demonstrated that the intellectual and perceptual development of children in late childhood, severely afflicted with cerebral palsy and who lacked the capacity to move with any effectiveness, were equal to children with the ability to move normally (1).

Vision seems critical to the learning and performance of most motor skills. So-called kinesthetic learning (blindfolding the participant) of various sports skills has usually produced inconclusive or negative results. One recent investigation demonstrated that an individual can learn a motor skill involving one hand just as well by observing another perform the skill as he can by first learning it himself with his opposite hand (9).

On the other hand there is a vast amount of evidence that limiting the visual experiences of animals and children seriously limits their intellect. Cultural deprivation studies are examples of those from which this evidence might be obtained. Similarly studies carried out with animals indicate that measurable differences in the biochemical make-up of the brain and in brain weight are elicited in animals who are exposed to environments which are visually stimulating (10).

One Saturday last year we spent the day testing two little girls; identical twins, thirteen years of age. One had been blind since birth. The data obtained during the course of this investigation supplied further insights into the interactions between vision and movement.

Despite the fact that the blind twin was extremely bright (I.Q. about 180), could write poetry, was an accomplished singer, and was free from any measurable emotional difficulties, when asked to run or to throw a ball she demonstrated marked ineptitude. She had not had the opportunity to "braille" another child running or throwing, as indeed it is impossible to do. It appeared that many children's movement patterns are probably copies from their peers, and the extent to which this "pick-up" of movement patterns has been accomplished is probably dependent upon the child's ability to organize his visual world.

This kind of finding might lead one to speculate that perhaps many of the movement problems evidenced by the neurologically handicapped child may stem not only from defects in his neuromotor mechanisms, but also might be caused by problems involving visual perceptions which prevent him from effectively organizing and copying the movements of other children and adults with whom he is engaged at play.

PERCEPTION VERSUS LEVERS AND PULLEYS

Findings from our research with the blind has given us insight into the role of perception in the formation of gross movement patterns. After observing both the blind and the blindfolded sighted attempting to walk straight on a large athletic field without external cues, several things became apparent. Despite a general similarity in the lever and pulley systems of all human beings, individual differences in movement are most amenable to elucidation by reference to psychological variables rather than by an examination of the physics of movement.

For years the literature has assumed that the tendency of humans to spiral when deprived of external cues was dependent upon the fact that about 70 per cent of us have a short leg. However, we found that leg length had no relationship to the direction or to the magnitude of veer and spiral evidenced by our subjects. People walked, in our investigation, where they *thought* they should, not where their legs walked them! Humans are not little wind-up toys who will go where you point them; rather they are thinking, feeling, verbal animals, constantly surrounded by a constellation of motives which are usually in a state of flux. To attempt to predict movements, either their intensity or their configurations, or indeed whether an individual will choose to perform a task or not without reference to various psychological parameters of behavior is a superficial approach to the study of the complexities of the human action system (2,7).*

The training arising from this kind of finding was based upon giving the blind a cognitive awareness of the amount and direction of their veer and by enabling them to inspect tactually a model containing a flexible wire which could be bent to describe the shape of the pathway they had walked on previous trials. Mobility trainers of the blind have for years attempted to correct the veering tendency of their charges by placing lifts under the heel of the short leg. How many practices in physical education are equally superficial, short-sighted, and based upon similar incorrect assumptions?

PERSONAL EQUATIONS IN MOVEMENT

Evidence obtained when the blind were asked to make

*Additional evidence supporting the hypothesis that some kind of perceptual assymetry molds veering was the tendency noted for the subjects, when attempting to draw a straight line at right angles to the front of their bodies to veer their arm away from their body, in the *same* direction as they veered when attempting to walk straight on the athletic field!

facing movements gave further information relative to a personal equation in movement. When the blind (and also the sighted) are asked to make facing movements without auditory or visual cues available, they tend to overturn the 90 degree turns requested, while underturning 180 degree turns by about 10 degrees and underturning full turns that were asked for by about 40 degrees!

Other evidence indicates that when asked to draw lines 4 inches long, individuals will draw them longer than four inches, and when asked for 15-inch lines, subjects will usually draw a line shorter than this. In other terms there seem to be certain types of preferences involving the amount of space a person wishes to use in various movement tasks relatively independent of the instructions extended.

Similar personal equations have been researched involving habitual force in movements, preferred speed of movements, persistence in movements, as well as personal preferences for various rhythmic patterns in movement. These studies are not plentiful, but they form a fascinating and important part of the experimental literature and elucidate a classification of qualities which without doubt influence the performance and learning of tasks within the experimental laboratory as well as on the playfield.

ANXIETY AND PERFORMANCE

The critical role of anxiety in the formation of movement attributes was also demonstrated to us when examining some of the data arising from our studies of the blind. Attempting to acertain some of the variables which contributed to the veering tendency, scores of subjects scoring 0 or 1 on Taylor's scale of anxiety were compared to the amount of veer evidenced by subjects scoring above 8 on Taylor's 20-point scale of manifest anxiety.

The low anxiety subjects walked faster (4 feet per second, as compared to 3 feet per second), veered only about 11 feet per 100 feet of travel, as compared to 23 feet of veer evidenced by the more highly anxious subjects. Thus veer was dependent upon the personality of the subject, the time during which the task was engaged in, and the distance the subjects walked. It is probable that marked differences in performance caused by anxiety are reflected in a variety of perceptual-motor skills of importance to the special educator and the physical educator.

It is frequent to note, for example, the influence of emotional states upon the child's ability to write accurately and rapidly. Emotional problems frequently manifest themselves in residual tension in the hands; the hands are the outlet for a child's intellect, and if they are not functioning properly, an irrevocable chain of tension-hand-writing-failure-tension-further failure is set in motion.

...AND THE RETARDED TEACH US COGNITION

Data coming from an evaluation of the perceptual-motor functioning of the retarded have also afforded us insight into basic questions pertinent to the normal as well as to the atypical child. Severely retarded children seldom give evidence of abstract symbolic thought, so the quantity of their motoric behavior *is the only* evidence that we may obtain of their thought process (2).

MOTIVATION AND PERFORMANCE

Analysis of developmental trends in a variety of perceptual-motor measures elicited from educable retardates and from the neurologically handicapped provide important information relative to motivation. These children's scores were *best* at about the age of twelve with a decline in ability noted after late childhood had been reached (subjects up to the age of twenty-four years were tested). Performance of the normal youth tends to "peak" at about sixteen in the case of girls, and at about eighteen to nineteen in the case of boys in our culture.

It is reasonable to assume that these atypical children begin during late childhood, as they become aware of their ineptitudes, to withdraw from participation in vigorous activities. This withdrawal further lowers their capacities to participate which results in the evidence cited.

WORK METHODS AND PERFORMANCE OF SKILLS

Seashore devoted an entire chapter to the importance of "work methods" to motor skill performance in the 1951 *Handbook of Experimental Psychology* (S.S. Stevens, Ed.). It is difficult when evaluating retarded youngsters to determine whether ineptitudes uncovered are due to basic neuromotor deficiencies or whether the children simply select an inappropriate method for performing the task. Experimentalists often make the naive assumption that their subjects will follow their directions rather than devising unique and at times unexpected methods for accomplishing the task at hand.

Retardates were sometimes noted, for example, when asked to stand on one leg, to assume a posture with both legs wide-spread and then attempt unsuccessfully to lift one. Their balance score was low, not because of a defect in their balance mechanisms, but because they selected a poor method of accomplishing a one-foot balance.

Performance of skill by the normal or the atypical youngster is the result of a combination of experience, ingenuity in devising appropriate procedures, and basic physical capacities. The physical educator should be cognizant of this triad of causative factors and attempt to instill the most appropriate work methods at opportune times within the learning process, commensurate with the ability of the child to understand the task at hand.

SPECIFICITY VERSUS GENERALITY OF SKILL

A frequent debate when researchers interested in motor learning collect data is whether skill is specific or general. Experimental evidence usually gives lie to the common observation that there are generally well-coordinated people who seem to perform a variety of skills well. I recently attempted to devise a conceptual framework to attempt to reconcile the discrepancy between what is observed and what is measured in the experimental laboratory (4).

Data obtained this summer from our work with the

retarded gave support to the importance of the nature of the capacities of the subjects, when attempting to ascertain whether skill is specific or general (4). The correlation matrices based upon six perceptual-motor categories evidenced increased specificity as a function of increased intellect. For example, the average intercorrelation between the scores obtained from trainable retardates (I.Q. 30-50) was .52, a common variance of about 27 per cent. On the other hand educable retardates (I.Q. about 70) produced scores whose average intercorrelation was only .32, common variance of about 10 per cent. Intercorrelations of tests of mental ability to measures of perceptual-motor ability evidence the same increase as a function of I.Q.

Not only do such findings lead to important implications when devising educational programs for the retarded, but also they provide insight into the nature of the development of human behavior on the part of normal children. This differentiation of function by normal children is often alluded to in the clinical and experimental literature, although not as frequently accommodated for in educational programs for the preschool youngster.

CONCLUSIONS

It seems to me that the evidence cited brings results in several conclusions. Not only can we in physical education make important contributions to man's general knowledge about himself by carrying out penetrating studies of behavior elicited by various neural and/or biochemical malfunctions, but we can also make important contributions to the education of children with a greater variety of problems than have attracted our interest in the past. Formerly, only our adapted physical educators were interested in the orthopedically handicapped, the structurally malformed child.

If we consider ourselves competent in the area of motor functioning, then we should also be ready to provide program guidelines in the form of research evidence to those interested in improving the perceptual-motor behaviors of the neurologically handicapped, the emotionally disturbed, and the retarded. If we consider ourselves knowledgeable in the perception of movement—kinesthesis—we should then stand ready to aid individuals who rely to a large extent upon tactual-kinesthetic cues; the blind.

Our suggestions to the special educator must not be based upon emotionally laden speculations, but upon solid experimental evidence translatable into programs of education. We must be ready to communicate to groups who can utilize our data, to get down on the floor with the mongoloid child to demonstrate the influence of balance training upon his total functioning.

Proceeding from a scholarly interest, to a research effort, to program implementation, should make us valuable to the total community of typical and atypical children as well as enhancing our images within the professional communities and in institutions of higher learning. We will achieve progress in our understanding of the movement behavior of humans by thinking, collecting data, then acting and demonstrating how others might act in constructive ways.

REFERENCES

1. Abercrombie, M.L.J.; Gardiner, P.A.; Hansen, E.; Jonckheere, J; Lindon, R.L.; Solomon, G., and Tyson, M.C.: Visual, perceptual and visuomotor impairment in physically handicapped children. *Percept Motor Skills* (Monogr. Suppl.), 3-V18, 1964.
2. Cratty, Bryant J.: Perceptual thresholds of non-visual locomotion (Part I, Monogr.). Department of Physical Education, University of California, Los Angeles, August 1965.
3. Cratty, Bryant J: A three level theory of perceptual-motor behavior. *Quest*, VI:3, May 1966.
4. Cratty, Bryant J.: The perceptual-motor attributes of mentally retarded children and youth (Monogr.). Mental Retardation Services Board of Los Angeles County, August 1966.
5. Cratty, Bryant J., and Hutton, Robert S.: Figural aftereffects resulting from gross action patterns. *Res Quart*, 35:2, 1964.
6. Cratty, Bryant J., and Williams, Harriet G.: Accuracy of facing movements executed without vision. *Percept Motor skills*, 23:1231, 1966.
7. Cratty, Bryant J., and Williams, Harriet G.: Perceptual thresh-

olds of non-visual locomotion (Monogr.). Department of Physical Education, University of California, Los Angeles, 1966.

8. Dennis, Wayne: Infant development under conditions of restricted practice and of minimum social stimulation. *Genet Psychol Monogr., 23:*143, 1941.

9. Eberhard, Ulrich: Transfer of training related to finger dexterity. *Percept Motor Skills, 17:*274, 1963.

10. Eiduson, Samuel; Eiduson, B.T.; Geller, Edward, and Yuwiler, Arthur: *Biochemistry and Behavior,* Princeton, Van Nostrand, 1964.

B. Blind Children and Youth

Chapter 16

THE DEVELOPMENT OF PERCEPTUAL-MOTOR ABILITIES IN BLIND CHILDREN AND YOUTH

I WOULD FIRST like to attempt to define some of the terms contained in the title of this presentation. The word *perception* has many meanings and to examine even some of them now would not permit us to keep within our time limit. Fortunately, the hyphenated term *perceptual-motor* has more limited meaning and is usually an adjective applied to a motor skill whose execution is heavily dependent upon the accuracy with which the performer organizes incoming sensory information. With reference to blind children, perceptual-motor behavior may refer to their efforts to learn by manually inspecting various components of their environment or, in a broader context, to movements which enable them to judge their ever-changing position in space while walking.

The phrase *blind children and youth* also needs some explanation. An authority on blindness has recently suggested that *blind* must be considered in the plural. He states that one must differentiate between the blind from birth and those who have become blind through some kind of disease or accident; the adventitiously blind. This same author also presents a second dichotomy, with which to classify the blind; the rehabilitated blind versus those who emotionally have not come to terms with their affliction (2).

This morning we will focus our attention primarily upon the judgments important to the blind while they walk.

Speech given at the eighth Annual Research Program on Exceptional Children and Youth, sponsored by the University of California, Extension, June 30, 1966.

Most of the blind children and youth who have been our subjects are relatively well adjusted, intelligent, and have been blind since birth.

For several years prior to our work with the blind, we conducted basic investigations of human performance and learning in which the sighted subjects' vision was frequently eliminated by blindfolding them in order to better control sensory input. It became apparent while working on these studies that some of the information we were obtaining could have practical significance for the blind. Two years ago we initiated a five-year program in which we hoped to determine some of the variables which contribute to the accurate mobility of the sightless.

It is extremely difficult for the sighted to place themselves within the reference system employed by the person who has never had vision. While the blind from birth are frequently heard to utter "sighted" terms such as "red" and "shiny," it is doubtful whether these words are anything but interesting adjectives applied to certain nouns. If queried about their conception of color, for example, the sightless child will sometimes say "The sky is blue, the grass is green," but colors are sighted terms.

Unless presented with increasingly complex objects to manually inspect, the blind child may fall intellectually behind the sighted child. Particular difficulty may be noted as the blind child attempts to grasp concepts related to space. A forty-two year old man blind from birth recently told me of the great difficulty he had grasping the concept "fifteen feet away."

Just as it is difficult to understand the blind, it is not until about the age of four or five that many blind children begin to realize that the rest of us are different in an important way for them. One blind twin pair was reported by their mother as first realizing that there was something different about her sensory system when they failed to "hide" from her, as they could from each other, by becoming silent. Another report regarding the age of this discovery stated that not until seven did a blind girl perceive she was somehow different as she discovered that her mother was able to identify a friend in a nearby car, while she could not. (12).

There are basic philosophical and practical questions which arise, or should arise, when educational and recreational programs are designed for blind children. Should they be treated simply as sighted children who cannot see? or are there basic perceptual, intellectual, and emotional differences to be considered in their make-up? For example, it is usually believed desirable to eliminate "blindisms" evidenced by children blind from birth; the rocking movements and other rhythmic motoric behaviors evidenced as the blind child engages in apparently pleasurable self-stimulation. To the sighted, however, this kind of behavior is unpleasant to observe, and as it usually is felt that its continuance will impede the blind child socially, it is trained out of him—but to be replaced by what?

From scientific and semi-scientific writings concerning these and other questions, various spurious assumptions have arisen during the past years. Some of these have been put to chase by research while others persist.

For example, the fabled obstacle sense of the blind has been reasonably well documented as having its genesis in reflected auditory cues. The more recent suggestion in popular magazines that there are certain blind people who can judge color through their fingertips is another example. I had brief contact with this fable two years ago when I was asked to design a proposal to determine whether the tactile perception of color was possible. My review of the literature on the manual perception of roughness and of heat brought me to the conclusion, prior to beginning the study, that the identification of colors through the fingertips was impossible. Fortunately the research was never consummated, for I also learned at about this same time from two Russian psychologists that the Russian woman who claimed to possess this magical power had later admitted to looking under her blindfold!

Intelligent children blind from birth often possess abilities which are remarkably uneven in nature when compared to attributes evidenced by the sighted. For example, they frequently exhibit extensive vocabularies but are not really sure of the nature of a traffic intersection. They may be able to read braille but have great difficulty signing their name in script. A study comparing a blind and sighted identical twin pair recently completed in our laboratory revealed that, despite the blind girl's high intellect, she had only a vague concept of the human face; she could not throw nor run accurately; and when asked to draw "her favorite thing" could inscribe only a vague outline of her pet parakeet (11).

Overall educational programs for blind children seem reasonably adequate during the middle years of childhood. Blind children enter school at about the age of five and learn braille as well as other traditional subjects. By the age of thirteen they can read and write braille adequately and usually graduate to junior high school where they continue their studies.

The more marked deficiencies in the total educational program for blind children are in two areas: (a) pre-primary preparation for the complexities of classroom learning, and (b) preparation which will enable them to become mobile and self-sufficient in their environment during and after their school years.

Mobility training° for the blind received its major impetus during World War II and continued after this time to present programs primarily for adults. While traditionally educational programs for the sighted are designed to begin at about the fifth year of age, the blind child generally does not receive any mobility training prior to the age of sixteen or eighteen. Guide dogs are not given to children as it is believed they are not able to continue their training, but will make them relatively useless by rewarding their pets with too much affection.

Not until the past two or three years have major efforts been made to organize programs for training blind children to become safely mobile in their homes, neigh-

---

°Mobility training is a program of education designed to facilitate the safe and accurate travel of the blind in the city streets through the use of the cane and/or dog, by attempting to aid them to organize auditory, tactile, and kinesthetic cues supplied by environmental noise, and various sensory extensions.

borhood, and in their communities despite the fact that
safe mobility seems to be one of the keys to self-suffi-
ciency and mental health on the part of the blind. At this
time these programs are only in the planning phases, and
in most communities in which they are contemplated they
are not expected to begin for several more years.

A review of the literature relating to data upon which
these mobility training programs were established led me
to the conclusion that in most cases they employed techniques which were unsupported by objective evidence. The
tendency for the blind to veer, for example, while frequently observed, had not been measured.° While investi-
gators had studied the ability of rats to perceive gradient
changes without vision, no effort had been made to evaluate this ability on the part of humans without sight.

It is with these considerations in mind that the research program was initiated. During the first year, we
obtained basic normative data and from this constructed
a mobility orientation test. This test measures an individual's ability to detect gradient and to walk straight
without vision. Norms were compiled by assessing others
similar in age. During the second year of the investigation,
we have attempted to ascertain the effects of brief practice upon various perceptual attributes. During the next
three years, if our support continues, we intend to explore
the effect of auditory cues upon the accurate mobility of
blind children, youth, and adults. During the initial year
of this investigation about 180 subjects were utilized including forty-five children and youth from the ages of eight
to nineteen. During the second year of the investigation we
employed fewer subjects, but detained them for two days
during which various kinds of tests were administered.

Essentially it is believed that our findings will not
only tend to encourage mobility trainers to examine more
closely some of their traditional practices but will also
tend to facilitate communication between the blind and the
sighted by aiding each to better understand the reference
system of the other. For example, it was found that while
the sighted can easily detect horizontal deviations in the
direction a blind individual is taking while attempting to

walk a straight line, the blind are many times more sensitive to gradient changes than are the sighted visually inspecting the same surfaces. Similarly the curvature of curbs which are obviously curved when the sighted inspect them are difficult, if not impossible, to detect by the blind employing the cane techniques presently advocated by mobility trainers.

Mobility trainers have at times placed heel lifts under the leg toward which the blind trainee veers, while our findings suggest in several ways that the veering tendency is caused by some kind of perceptual distortion, rather than by structure. The blind, just as do the sighted, walk their legs; their legs do not walk them! A most interesting finding is that the direction an individual will habitually veer on the field can be predicted by asking him to draw a "straight" line directly away from the center of his body while seated at a table.

Further evidence which has important implications for the perceptual-motor development and training of blind children was gained as they were asked to walk through the curved twenty-foot pathways with radii ranging from twelve to forty-two feet. Sixty per cent of the responses obtained from children blind from birth were inaccurate, whereas the adventitiously blind were usually correct in their judgements of these pathways. As the blind from birth were more accurate when walking straight and were also more accurate than the adventitiously blind when judging gradient, one might conclude that these children blind from birth did not have an accurate concept of laterality firmly established. Their ability to differentiate between left and right was extremely poor.

Most child development experts suggest that the child's basic perceptions of his body are formed early, including an awareness of its surfaces as well as perception of the differences in the sides of the body. By the age of six, it is usually suggested the child's laterality as evidenced by hand use is well established. It was apparent

---

*The tendency to veer and to spiral in the absence of orienting cues has been evidenced by amoeba, mice and a number of mammals including man.

from our data that in the case of the blind-from-birth, laterality was not well established.

These kinds of data suggest that in addition to an orderly presentation of increasingly complex objects to manually inspect, the child blind from birth should also be given training rather early in life designed to heighten his awareness of his body parts. Probably such training should accompany, and may enhance, the development of speech.

As soon as possible the infant should be made aware of his front and back, and parts of his face, and the location and name of his limbs. Furthermore he should be, in every possible way, given tasks designed to enable him to understand various left-right concepts; that his left and right changes as he moves, and that an individual facing him has a different left and right than he does. At the same time the child should be made to understand that his left arm and leg emerge from the left side of his body and be given tasks which enable him to locate himself relative to various objects. Using a box, for example, various drills may be utilized which might help him to understand how to stand with his back, his front, his left side, and his right side nearest an object. If we are to believe the writings of Piaget regarding the importance of the sensory-motor period in the development of an infant and the sensory-tonic theory of perception advanced by Werner, it would seem that this kind of body-image training is imperative for the child who has no opportunity to pair vision with movement (8,10).

In other ways the child can be taught a concept of *straightness* when traveling. Utilizing the flexible wire (experiment described in Chapter 18), the child can begin to gain an accurate concept of the pathway he is taking as his walking develops. Through the use of models he can begin to gain a concept of street intersections and of safe and unsafe crossing conditions.

Auditory training, as outlined in the research by Norton, can also be employed early in the life of the child (5). Sounds can be paired with objects and with specific rooms in the home. At the same time sounds can be utilized to heighten the child's spatial orientation by placing them at various angles around him. Our intention during the next three years is, with the help of researchers in the departments of psychology and otology, to investigate the manner in which stable and moving sound cues contribute to and detract from the child's ability to move accurately, to detect obstacles, and in other ways to deal with his environment.

The electronic obstacle detection device invented by Dr. Kay in England is being experimented with at M.I.T. and at the Catholic Center for All the Blind in Newton, Massachusetts. At the present time it is expected that this device must be used with the traditional cane. It is intended, however, to permit children to grow up with them in order that they may gain a better concept of the nature of their world.

It is thus believed that three basic improvements are needed in the educational programs for blind children: early and thorough tactile training, using objects of various degrees of complexity; systematic "body-image" training affording the blind child a better concept of his body, its location relative to objects, its parts, and its left-right dimensions; and a program of mobility education started as soon as the child begins to walk. It is believed that through this three-pronged effort, more blind children will arrive at school emotionally prepared to participate in formal programs of education and will emerge from school intellectually prepared to make meaningful contributions to society.

REFERENCES

1. Burlingham, D.: Some notes on the development of the blind, *Psychoanal Stud Child*, 16:121, 1954.
2. Carroll, Rev. Thomas J.: *Blindness*. Boston, Little, 1961.
3. Cratty, Bryant J.: Perceptual thresholds of non-visual locomotion. I. The veering tendency, the perception of gradient and of curvature in pathways: Interrelationships, norms, inter-group comparisons and a mobility orientation test. Department of Physical Education, Universty of California at Los Angeles, August 1965.

4. Cratty, Bryant J., and Williams, Harriet G.: Perceptual thresh-olds of non-visual locomotion. II. The effects of brief prac-tice upon veer, upon accuracy of facing movements and upon position relocation. The perception of lateral tilt in pathways walked and of curvature of curbs. The relation-ship of accuracy of performance in selected tabletop draw-ing tasks to the veering tendency and to position relocation. Department of Physical Education, University of Califor-nia at Los Angeles, June 1966.
5. Norton, Fay-Tyler M.: *Training Hearing to Greater Usefulness* (Manual). Cleveland Society for the Blind, 1960.
6. Parmalee, Arthur H., Jr.: Developmental studies of blind chil-dren. I. *The New Outlook for the Blind.* The American Foundation for the Blind, June, 1966.
7. Parmalee, H.A.; Fiske, C.E., and Wright, R.H.: The development of ten children with blindness as a result of retrolental fibroplasia. *Dis Child, 98:*198, 1959.
8. Piaget, Jean: *The Construction of Reality in the Child.* New York, Basic Books, 1954.
9. Shilling, C.W.: Identification and teaching of auditory cues for traveling in the blind. (Final progress report). C. W. Shill-ing Auditory Research Center, Groton, March 1963.
10. Werner, H., and Wapner, W.: Sensory-tonic field theory of per-ception. *J Personality, 18:*88, 1949.
11. Williams, Harriet G., and Beane, Virginia: A comparison of se-lected behaviors of a pair of identical twins, one blind from birth. Submitted for publication in *Children.*
12. Wolff, Peter: Developmental studies of blind children. II. *The New Outlook for the Blind.* The American Foundation for the Blind, June 1966.

Chapter 17

MOBILITY RESEARCH AT UCLA
A Summary and Implications of the Findings

INTRODUCTION

OUR RESEARCH with the blind at UCLA grew out of basic investigations of human performance in which the subjects were usually blindfolded while attempting to learn mazes of various sizes. During the three-year course of this program, about six hundred blindfolded collegians participated as subjects. Not only were data such as traversal speed inspected, but the subjects were also polled concerning their subjective feelings when in these experimental situations (2).

Reports of this nature gave rise to further research exploring what the psychologists term *kinesthetic, or figural aftereffects of movement*. For example, after some subjects traversed large mazes, they would frequently talk about curves which in reality did not exist. At other times, they would fail to draw irregularities in a pathway which were actually present. The turns in these pathways seemed to elicit various illusions of movement (4).

Further research on these basic problems involved the construction of short pathways formed in the shape of half-circles and straight lines. After walking several times in pathways requiring left turns, the blindfolded subjects would report that straight pathways were actually curved in the direction opposite to that they had initially walked. Similar investigations created distortions of gradient.

While carrying out these studies, it became apparent that a pathway had to have a radius of about 18 feet before a blindfolded subject walking through it would consistently report its curvature. There seemed to be a threshold to curvature which had to be exceeded.

It was at this point that we consulted research dealing with the perceptions of the blind in order to ascertain whether this kind of measure had been experimentally identified. During this same period we also visited mobility training programs around the Los Angeles area and talked to the trainers and to their blind clients regarding basic questions. With the encouragement of these two groups we then initiated the applied research project we will be discussing here.

PERIPATOLOGY PROJECT

During the initial year of our project, supported by the National Institute of Neurological Diseases and Blindness, about two hundred blind subjects were contacted through various agencies and brought to the campus in order to obtain basic data dealing with the veering tendency, the perceptions of gradient, and the perceptions of curvature in short pathways. During this initial year we also collected basic structural data involving the measurement of leg length and of postural imbalances (3).

During the second year of the project, just completed, fewer subjects were utilized, but more measures were obtained. Forty-five subjects ranging in age from seventeen to fifty-five years spent two entire days with our research staff. The data collected during this second year consisted of extensions of the measures obtained during the initial year as well as supplementary measures which it was believed would better elucidate some of the phenomena observed initially (6). Emphasis during the second year was placed upon the effects of brief training upon some of the attributes important to the mobility of the blind.

Several basic criteria governed the administration of these tests. In line with a sound application of the scientific method of problem solving, the evaluations were arranged so that the influence of only one variable at a time was considered as influencing the attribute. For example, when evaluating the veering tendency, subjects' ears were plugged due to the inability to adequately control the variety of noises to which the subjects might be exposed. It was hypothesized that while the blind obviously depend upon sound cues when mobile, the sensory information which is always present in a reasonably consistent form are cues arising from the movements of their muscles when walking and from their vestibular apparatus. We will be able in future years to study the influence of various auditory environments upon various mobility problems, the ability to locate obstacles, as well as the ability to utilize "auditory shadows" in the environment.

THE FINDINGS

It was found that the blind do indeed veer in a reasonably consistent direction at the rate of from 25 degrees to 75 degrees per 100 feet of forward travel attempted. On the average they swerved about 1.24 inches per step. This veering seems caused by some kind of perceptual distortion, rather than by structure and can be partially arrested by giving the individual an exact awareness of the direction and the amount of his usual veering pattern.

The walking speed of the individual as well as his general level of anxiety were related to the amount of veer evidenced. Subjects walking at about three feet per second veered about twice as much at one hundred feet as did subjects walking at about four feet per second. At the same time individuals scoring in the upper quartile in a test of anxiety veered significantly more and walked significantly slower than subjects who scored in the lower quartile of this anxiety scale (11).

The older individual, newly blind, veered considerably more than did the youth and adult blind from birth. The amount of veer evidenced by individuals seems dependent upon the extent to which they attend to the task of walking straight and how long they attempt to maintain a straight course. The longer the time they walk, the more they veer. Individuals veer immediately if asked simply to *walk* in the absence of orienting cues. The subjects veer after walking about one hundred feet if they are asked to *walk a straight line* and are given some idea of what that *straight line* initially *feels like*. On the other hand, if people are given some instruction in the form of the tabletop grids, concerning the direction and amount of veer they evidenced on a previous trial, they tend to walk about 200 feet before evidencing the tendency to veer and/ or to spiral.

The subjects were found to be most sensitive to walking a declining surface (threshold about one degree) and less sensitive to walking up hill or on a surface slanted to the right or to the left (thresholds about 2 degrees in the latter three instances). It appeared that a pathway had to have a radius of about forty feet before the subjects could be counted upon to report curvature with more accuracy than could be expected by chance.

A most exciting finding was the indication that the perceptual distortion of straightness was reflected in a tabletop task in which the subject attempted to draw a straight line directly away from the center of his body. About 90 per cent of the time the direction the subjects were found to consistently veer on an athletic field was predictable by knowing the direction they usually veered their arm when attempting to draw a line on a desk (6).

Although no relationships were found between table-top veer and veering tendency evidenced in the gymnasium, it was felt that the true direction in which a subject was likely to veer was assessed with more accuracy on the athletic field. Frequently, for example, a subject would veer slightly to the left or right during his initial fifty or sixty feet on the field and then veer markedly in the opposite direction, maintaining the latter course for the remainder of his time on the field.

While it is believed that the above finding must be more thoroughly researched before it is completely understood, it does indicate that diagnosis of the veering tendency may be made within an economical amount of space.

While at the same time it is suggested that perhaps training the veering tendency *out* of an individual may be accomplished by spending at least part of the time with a pencil.

It was found that the curvature of curbs was not easily ascertained by drawing a cane along their surface, holding both general and specific implications for mobility trainers. While of course such a finding suggests that perhaps some techniques of this type might be reexamined, the finding also suggests that better communication between the blind and their trainers might be established if the latter attempted to place themselves within the "skin" of their clients with more frequency. In general, these and similar findings pointed to instances in which trainer-client communication might be facilitated if the former would attempt to better understand the perceptual limitations as well as the perceptual capacities of the latter.

A multiple correlation of +.55 was obtained upon comparing the veering tendency and the ability to make facing movements to the ability to relocate a position once occupied. This finding illustrated that truly "the sum of the parts equals the whole," and the best way to study the complexities of blind mobility is in analysis of components rather than by recourse to the kind of pragmatism frequently engaged in.

Both blind subjects and blindfolded-sighted controls, when asked to make various facing movements without the benefit of auditory cues, evidenced the same types of inaccuracies. Typically the subjects, when asked to turn 90 degrees, would turn farther—about 100 degrees. However, when asked to make one-half or full turns, they would characteristically underturn them; in the case of half-turns, this would amount to about 10 degrees. When asked to make full turns, however, the subjects would on the average only turn about 310 degrees (5).

The inaccuracy with which the subjects were able to make facing movements holds implications for the training of the blind. The inaccuracy with which the subjects executed 180 and 360-degree turns, for example, suggests that specific training in this attribute would be helpful prior to extensive work on the city streets in which frequent accurate facings are required.

FUTURE RESEARCH

The findings of this program point to innumerable avenues which future researchers might take. One which this investigator proposes to travel involves the addition of auditory cues of various kinds and the assessment of the accuracy with which various mobility problems can be accomplished under these kinds of conditions. For example, if our support continues, it is intended to place fixed sound sources at various positions around a field and to study mobility with sound at the front, rear, side(s), and in various combinations relative to the subjects' intended lines of travel.

Following research of this nature, with the assistance of colleagues in otology, psychology, and special education, it is intended to study mobility in the presence of various moving sound cues similar to those present as the blind traverse the sidewalks of our cities.

Various basic problems suggested by these findings may also be explored. For example, the manner in which table-top training may correct the veering tendency is a logical extension of this year's study. At the same time, models of various environments more complex than a simple straight pathway can be studied as possibly influential of accurate mobility. Various cane techniques now apparently acceptable due to their traditional use might also be evaluated under controlled experimental conditions.

A "wedding" between the program now being conducted by Dr. Rice at Stanford University relative to the approach utilized by this investigator might be arranged (8). For example, in a large area in which the auditory environment may be exactly described and controlled, the obstacle sense of the blind as well as their facility in dealing with auditory shadows could be thoroughly explored. Through such cooperative research, this kind of experimental situation could be made increasingly complex so that eventually it would resemble conditions found in the "real world."

REFERENCES

1. Bauman, Mary K.: *A Comparative Study of Personality Factors in Blind, Other Handicapped, and Non-Handicapped Individuals.* Washington, D.C. U.S. Office of Vocational Rehabilitation Service Series No. 134, 1950.
2. Cratty, Bryant J.: Assessing movement accuracy with a fluid-patterned locomotor maze. *Percept Motor Skills, 13:*162, 1961.
3. Cratty, Bryant, J.: Perceptual thresholds of non-visual locomotion Monogr., Part I. Department of Physical Education, University of California, Los Angeles, August 1965.
4. Cratty, Bryant J., and Hutton, Robert S.: Figural aftereffects resulting from gross action patterns. *Res Quart 35:*2, 1964.
5. Cratty, Bryant J., and Williams, Harriet G.: Accuracy of facing movements executed without vision. *Percept Motor Skills, 23:*1231, 1966.
6. Cratty, Bryant J.: Perceptual thresholds of non-visual locomotion (Monogr., Part II). Department of Physical Education, University of California, Los Angeles, 1966.
7. Cratty, Bryant J.: The "veering tendency" of the arm, when drawing a straight line without vision. Submitted to *Res Quart,* 1966.
8. Rice, C.E.; Feinstein, S.H., and Schusterman, R.J.: Echo detection ability of the blind: Size and distance factors. *J Exp Psychol, 70* (3):246, 1965.
9. Schaeffer, A.A.: Spiral movement in man. *J Morph, 45:*293, 1928.
10. Schilling, C.W.: Identification and teaching of auditory cues for traveling in the blind. (Final progress report). Groton, Conn., C.W. Schilling Auditory Research Center, March 1963.
11. Taylor, Janet A.: A personality test for manifest anxiety. *J Abnorm Soc Psychol, 48:*285, 1953.

Chapter 18

THE EDUCABILITY OF DYNAMIC SPATIAL ORIENTATIONS IN BLIND CHILDREN

THE PROBLEM of training the blind to move through their environment is met by a blind child as he learns to walk. Unfortunately, formal mobility training is available to very few blind teenagers throughout the country. It is important, however, to prepare blind children in various perceptual and perceptual-motor tasks which will enable them to take advantage of travel training when it is available.

For the past year, at the Frances Blend School in Los Angeles, we have attempted to incorporate two kinds of pre-mobility training into the curriculum. During the first three years (grades one through three), it is believed important to engage in training which aids the child to gain concepts relative to his body-image, his position in space relative to objects, his body parts and their movements, and if he is able, to make various left-right judgements about his body and his relationships to other things in his environment. A sixteen-step body-image sequence has been described elsewhere (see Chapter 23). This sequence has been found to be helpful by the teachers at the Blend School, and is presently undergoing further refinement using both blind and sighted children. During the final three years of elementary school, prior to entering junior high

This study was conducted by Mr. Carl Peterson at the Frances Blend Elementary School for the Blind in Los Angeles, California, in the spring of 1967. The writer and Mr. Peterson would like to express their thanks for the splendid cooperation extended to us by Miss Calone, Principal, and by her teaching staff who carried out the training described.

school, it is also believed that blind children may profit from training in the execution of more complex spatial judgements. It was with this in mind that research was undertaken during the spring of 1967 in which approximately thirty blind children from the age of seven to fourteen years of age participated. It was found in studies during the previous two years carried out by the writer that a score combining an assessment of veering accuracy and facing movement accuracy contributed about 30 per cent to what is termed position relocation in the blind (2,3). It thus was decided to initiate an eight-week training program in which both facing-movement practice, and straight-line walking practice would take place. It was hypothesized that practice in these tasks would result in significant improvement in the ability of blind children to relocate their position in space.[°]

The experimental group were students at the Frances Blend School for the Blind in Los Angeles, while the controls were obtained through the cooperation of the Foundation for the Junior Blind in Los Angeles. The latter group were tested and retested in the three tasks, with an eight-week period between testing sessions during which no training occurred. The experimental group had training in facing movements, and in veering (preventing veer when walking) twice a week for eight weeks. Each training session lasted approximately twenty minutes for each child and included four trials during which they attempted to walk a straight line for a distance of fifty feet, and twelve trials involving the execution of 90, 180, and 360-degree turns to both directions (4).

After each trial in the veering task during the training period, the child was permitted to touch a solder wire which had been bent to form the shape of the pathway he had actually traversed, and a solder wire which represented a straight path. These wires were contained in a small wooden square made of plywood. After each trial in

---

[°]Position relocation is measured by leading the child along the two sides of an isosceles triangle, and then requesting him to turn and return to his original position on the triangle by way of the hypotenuse. (The length of the hypotenuse in this study was 22 feet (5).

the facing-movement task during the training sessions, the child was manually corrected to the correct amount of turn by the teacher. The children were trained and tested individually. No training was received in the position-relocation problem, only a pre- and post-test was taken of this attribute (3).

The findings of this investigation were highly encouraging. Statistically significant improvement was made in both the veering task and in the facing-movement task by the experimental group. For example, they improved about 24 per cent in their ability to walk straight for a distance of fifty feet, an improvement in mean accuracy of about four feet of deviation for the distance traversed. The facing movements, particularly those involving a complete turn, also evidenced improvement which was significant.

Initially the children exhibited the characteristic tendency noted in previous studies to overturn 90-degree turns by about 7 degrees, and to underturn 180 and 360-degree turns (4); after training they were only, on the average, about 2 degrees in error when executing 90-degree turns, 4 degrees in error when making one-half turns, and about 10 degrees short when asked to make full turns.

Most importantly, it was clearly illustrated that the sum of the parts equals the whole, in so far as training in two of the components of the ability to locate one's position in space without the use of vision (veering and facing movements) elicited a significant improvement in the former task. Following eight weeks of training as described, the children evidenced a significantly improved ability to locate their position in space in the task described. Initially in two trials the children evidenced a mean error of twenty-five feet; after training the mean error was only nineteen feet from their original starting points. In addition to the improvement reflected in these statistics, other more positive outcomes were noted on the part of children by the teachers who participated in this research training program. For example, the children were easily oriented through verbal directions while on the playground. Children did not have to be led in if they became disoriented at the completion of recess, but could be called upon to make a 90-degree turn and walk straight.

The children's concepts of left and right were also enhanced through the training in facing movements. During the initial testing it was quite apparent that a large percentage of the children evidenced no clear-cut concept of laterality. At the completion of the training, however, most could correctly turn to the right and left, and otherwise could make these spatial judgements about themselves and about objects in their environment.

With a coming of the spatial concepts inherent in the training program, several teachers noted that some of the children began to form more clear-cut perceptions of world geography. A knowledge of left and right about their bodies made it easier to conceptualize about latitude and longitude while they brailled the large globes available to them.

The results of this program were encouraging and indicate the feasibility of training blind children in basic perceptual judgements important to their mobility and to their basic interactions with the world. It is believed that this kind of training should precede the formal mobility training involving the use of the cane, auditory cues, etc. which should occur in secondary school.

REFERENCES

1. Cratty, Bryant J., and Sage, Jack N.: Spirokinesis. *Res Quart* 37 (4):480, 1966.
2. Cratty, Bryant J.: Perceptual thresholds of non-visual locomotion, Part I (Monogr.). Department of Physical Education, University of California at Los Angeles, 1965.
3. Cratty, Bryant J., and Williams, Harriet G.: Perceptual thresholds of non-visual locomotion, Part II (Monogr.). Department of Physical Education, University of California at Los Angeles, 1966.
4. Cratty, Bryant J.: Accuracy of facing movements executed without vision. *Percepi Motor Skills, 23:*1231, 1966.
5. Worchel, Philip: Space perception and orientation in the blind. *Psychol Monogr.,* 332:1, 1951.

C. The Clumsy Child Syndrome

Chapter 19

PRINCIPLES OF PERCEPTUAL-MOTOR TRAINING FOR CHILDREN WITH MINIMAL NEUROLOGICAL HANDICAPS

T HE VALUE of an educational program can only be assessed indirectly, by measuring changes in the desired behaviors of the participants. Therefore to properly assess the effectiveness of educational programs for children with minimal perceptual-motor problems, one must first ascertain what components of their motoric functioning are deficient, expose them to tasks which would seem to rectify these deficiencies and then retest them. Therefore our first job is to ascertain just what it is that these kind of children can or cannot do which interferes with their effective functioning in and with various components of their environment.

Fortunately, two recent investigations using a combined total of about 150 neurologically handicapped children have been carried out, producing findings which begin to delineate the general and specific perceptual-motor deficits which should probably be attended to when program planning (1,3). Jean Ayres, in a factor analysis published in 1965, identified five general areas of perceptual-motor dysfunction as the result of exposing 100 children with suspected dysfunction to a battery of thirty-five tasks.

The factors identified included the following:
1. *Body image deficit.* This factor is reflected in tasks involving the ability to duplicate accurate bodily and hand movements, and in tasks requiring the accurate

---

Paper delivered at the Pathway School Institute, Washington D.C., May, 1967.

localization of fingers, and in other tests of tactile perception. The factor loadings suggested that hand-finger "image" and body image are related attributes.

2. *Perceptual dysfunction: Lack of awareness of form and position in two-dimensional space.* This factor involves scores on tests evaluating the perception of form and position in space using both vision and tactile-kinesthetic cues without vision.

3. *Hyperactivity-distractibility.* This factor is identified by tasks indicating a deficit in tactile perception accompanied by hyperactive behavior. (Evidence of attempts to escape the testing situation with verbal and motor behavior was one measure contributing to this factor.)

4. *Integration of the two sides of the body.* Tests of rhythm and of the proficiency with which a child crosses his body (or attempts to avoid doing so) contribute to this factor.

5. *Figure-ground discrimination.* This is the inability to select superimposed figures out of confused backgrounds and similar tests.

6. *Balance.* This factor is obtained when tasks involving one-legged standing balance with eyes open and closed are analyzed.

While the majority of the tasks included in Ayres thirty-five battery test differentiated significantly between the 100 neurologically handicapped children and a control group of 50 "normals", it is interesting to note that the tests of mixed dominance involving hand-eye use revealed that this purported symptom of "perceptual disorganization" was as prevalent within the "normal" population as within the experimental group. Another finding which questions common "folklore" involved the lack of relationship found between left-right discrimination on the body and left-right decisions in visual space.

This latter finding might be explained by the seeming differentiation between bodily tonus and visual judgments revealed in the study carried out in 1957. Exploring the sensory-tonic theory of perception developmentally, it was found that bodily tonus seemed less related to spatial judgments in late childhood than was seen when younger children's bodily tonus was altered with the accompanying request to make accurate estimates of verticality (9).

The lack of congruence between the commonly held clinical assumption that cross-dominance accompanies neuromotor deficits reflected in learning problems may be explained by suggesting that such children simply accommodate to the inconvenience of dissimilar hand-eye preference, if indeed such a lack of hand-eye integration is really a critical problem at all.

In an investigation carried out last summer under the sponsorship of county, city and state agencies, approximately fifty children were evaluated in a variety of perceptual-motor tasks within six categories. These children ranged in age from five to nineteen years and had been classified as educationally handicapped by the Los Angeles City Schools (3). The findings of this study provide further guidelines for program planning.

It was found that only about one third evidenced atypical gait patterns while walking and crawling, although about two thirds failed to take a step with the proper foot when throwing. Moving backwards and laterally also proved difficult for these children, as did quickly arising from a back lying position on the mat.

In general, these children evidenced the most marked deficits in tasks involving the integration of movement with vision, including hand-eye, body-eye, or foot-eye coordination. Similar to the findings of Ayres, these data revealed that the children were unable to make various left-right discriminations about their body with accuracy. The findings of the "body-perception" category suggested a sixteen-step developmental sequence, which was later validated with a group of "normal" children at UCLA's University Elementary School.

The educationally handicapped children within the population studied exhibited motor competencies typical of well-functioning children from two to four years their juniors.

A striking finding with important implications for the early detection and alleviation of these perceptual-motor deficiences was revealed when the data was inspected upon a developmental continuum. The best performance scores were recorded by children between the ages of eleven and twelve within this population! It might be hypothesized that as these children meet frustrations and failure when attempting to function motorically, they withdraw from situations in which such competencies are needed, and this withdrawal further lowers capacities. This, of course, sets in motion a cycle of failure, perceived ineptitude, withdrawal from participation, lowering of capacity to perform, further failure, etc.

The score on the test battery most predictive of the total battery score was that obtained in the balance category. While at the same time intercorrelations between the various qualities evaluated revealed that these children function in rather specific ways. These data thus suggest that programs for the neurologically handicapped child contain several kinds of activities, rather than relying upon one or two "movement panaceas."

IMPLICATIONS FOR PROGRAM

The findings presented above could have been recited by every parent of a neurologically handicapped child without the aid of test batteries, Ph.D.'s and complex computers. The critical questions in the minds of parents concern the components of programs for the amelioration of these subtle and obvious deficits. Parents become trapped by several kinds of circumstances when seeking help for their children: the rather ambiguous terms which are applied by the members of various disciplines whom they consult, complex jargon usually representing relatively simple behavioral manifestations; the difficulty of determining the relative influence of environmental, emotional and structural factors upon the behavior evidenced; the supposition on the part of some that perhaps the child's problem is only transitory or may be eliminated with some kind of movement panacea similar to the curing of an infection through the administration of an antibiotic; and also by the variety of special schools, reading specialists, "educationalists," etc. who seem to be attracted to the "business" of "helping" children for reasons which are other than altruistic.

I believe programs for neurologically handicapped children should be based upon several principles. The components should be based upon the best experimental evidence available, rather than upon the blind acceptance of the unsubstantiated theoretical outpouring of some "movement messiah." The program should be under conditions which are motivating and relatively tension-free. The program should involve exposure to a number of movement tasks, encompassing those designed to enhance body-hand image, locomotor abilities, visual-motor integrations of hand-eye, body-eye, foot-eye, balances of various types (static and dynamic balancing), and those designed to lead toward useful classroom skills and socially desirable sports skills.

Table II contains two classifications: "Perceptual-Motor Categories," which involves various kinds of attributes which should be improved when possible, and "General Considerations." Although the list of "Perceptual-Motor Categories" contains eight constituents, this does not mean that all of these attributes should or can be incorporated into every program at a given time. Rather the instructor should attempt to select those which are appropriate to the assessed deficiencies of the children in his charge. It is also apparent that several of these categories overlap, and thus a single activity might result in the improvement of more than one attribute.

Along the left-hand side of Table II are placed what have been termed "General Considerations." These are basic principles which should be attended to by those in charge and which underly the performance of a variety of tasks. Within the squares in the center of the diagram are specific program suggestions, involving an integration of the attributes it is desired to improve with the "General Consideration" list on the left.

An important general consideration which has not been included on the charts involves what might be termed "movement differentiation." These children frequently evidence the inability to direct their tensions and energies in tasks in efficient and specific ways. Frequent residual tensions are often seen. A " spill-over" of inappropriate tension in one arm, for example, is often seen as the child engages in an activity with the other. Upper body tension may accompany the child's efforts when jumping. Attempts to throw "softly" may be made in vain. Whenever possible the individual working with these children should be sensitive to this general and basic problem, and attempt to educate them to focus appropriate tensions in the body parts being utilized in the task at hand, and to differentiate between the body parts in use and those not involved directly.

The general considerations should be incorporated into the program as follows:

Control. This implies that at times the child might be asked to move as slowly as he can, in an attempt to help him to place himself under his own control. Vigorous and rapid activity, while called for at times, will many times merely further excite the already excitable youngster.

Visual-Motor Pairing. When possible the child should be encouraged to involve visual control with his movements. Being asked to jump is not as productive as asking the child to jump with accuracy into a square, over a line, etc.

Segmental Integrations. The activities in the program should encourage the child to integrate the various bodily segments, to involve the top of his body with the bottom, and one side with the other. For example, proper arm involvement should be encouraged when jumping, and bilateral rhythmic activities should be encouraged to aid in left-right integration.

Decision Shifting. In line with "Control" above, when feasible, the child should be permitted to make decisions relative to the task, evaluation, etc. The theoretical framework presented by Mosston outlines in detail how this may be accomplished using perceptual-motor activities as a learning modality (8).

Social Complexity. Performance should be encouraged under conditions which gradually increase the complexity

TABLE II

GUIDELINES FOR A PERCEPTUAL-MOTOR TRAINING PROGRAM FOR CHILDREN WITH MINIMAL NEUROLOGICAL HANDICAPS

Perceptual-Motor Categories

General Considerations	Body-Hand Image	Balances	Locomotion	Agility	Finger-Hand-Eye Interactions	Strength, Endurance	Form and Movement Perception	Sports Skills
Control	Slowly move your hand while watching it.	See how slowly you can walk the line.	How slowly can you walk? how fast?	Can you stand up slowly?	How slowly can you draw a line?	Try fast pushups and then a slow one.	Trace around the figure slowly with your finger.	Run-and stop games.
Visual-Motor Pairing	Touch and look at your right hand with your left.	Watch the moving point while standing.	Jump into squares.	Roll and look at a point up there.	Place dots in the circles in time with the music.	Sit up and look at the X, now down and see the other.	Touch the ball swinging on the string as it passes you.	Let's play catch.
Segmental Integrations	Move your left hand and right leg at the same time.	Move down the beam using your arms to balance.	Jump using proper arm action.	Get up rapidly.	Tap rhythmically with one hand twice and then the other.	Hit with your left hand, while shifting body weight.	Trace a square with one hand and a circle with the other. Run and catch.	Rebounding in basketball is like this!
Decision Shifting	How many left-right things can you do?	How many ways can you walk the line?	How many ways can you jump into the box?	How can you get up? 6 ways?	How many ways can you draw a line from dot to dot?	Count and observe the form of his push-ups.	How many ways can you bounce the ball?	Can you invent a game with a stick?
Social Complexity	Touch your friend's right hand.	Follow the leader down the beam.	See how many ways your team can jump the line.	Let's have a hi-jump contest.	Bob, follow the line drawn by Jane on the board.	Let's have a push-up contest.	Bob, did Dick draw a triangle?	Now let's play with four on a side.

of social interactions and social *stress*. The child attempting to throw a ball to an adult therapist in an otherwise empty gymnasium is not comparable to playing catch with one's peers with the accompanying social punishment which may be received as the ball is dropped (5).

It has not been attempted to outline exact developmental sequences designed to enhance these attributes. I have attempted to do this in a one hundred-page paperback designed for parents and teachers (2). At the same time, it is believed that cognizance of these perceptual-motor categories and the manner in which they interact with general considerations should provide sound guidelines for the development of programs containing the relatively unsophisticated tasks a child with a minimal neurological handicap truly needs.

REFERENCES

1. Ayres, Jean: Patterns of perceptual-motor dysfunction in children: A factor analytic study, (Monogr. Suppl.). *Percept Motor Skills, I-V20:*335, 1965.
2. Cratty, Bryant J.: *Developmental Sequences of Perceptual-Motor Tasks.* Baldwin, New York, Educational Activities, 1967.
3. Cratty, Bryant J.: *The Perceptual-Motor Attributes of Mentally Retarded Children and Youth.* In cooperation with the Mental Retardation Services Board of Los Angeles County, August 1966.
4. Cratty, Bryant J.: *Movement Behavior and Motor Learning.* Philadelphia, Lea and F., 1967.
5. Cratty, Bryant J.: *Social Dimensions of Physical Activity.* Englewood Cliffs, Prentice-Hall, 1967.
6. Cratty, Bryant J.: *Psychology and Physical Activity.* Englewood Cliffs, Prentice-Hall, 1968.
7. Delacato, Carl H.: *The Diagnosis and Treatment of Speech and Reading Problems.* Springfield, Thomas, 1964.
8. Mosston, Muska: *Teaching Physical Education.* Columbus, Ohio, C. E. Merrill, 1966.
9. Wapner, S., and Werner, Heinz: *Perceptual Development, An Investigation Within the Framework of Sensory-Tonic Theory.* Clark U. Press, 1957.

Chapter 20

HYPERACTIVITY AND EDUCATION FOR PURPOSEFUL BEHAVIOR

HYPERACTIVITY is a common behavioral characteristic of many children who have been diagnosed as "brain damaged." These children seem totally unable to focus their attention for even a few moments, and the result is reflected in the inability to acquire basic concepts important to classroom learning, as well as severe distortion in their social relations with their peers and their parents. Six interrelated problems accompany this behavioral syndrome.

Distractibility

Children with this disorder evidence the marked inability to react to a single stimuli within their environment for even a brief period of time. They are stimulated by everything confronting them. Their attention is constantly redirected, with the result that learning is difficult. The least distraction refocuses their attention from the task at hand. This distractibility makes them extremely difficult to test.

When first observed, this behavior seems to be willed disobedience, and frequently the parents are admonished by teachers and others for failing to discipline their offspring. The problem, however, seems to depend upon the dysfunction of cortical control mechanisms which both inhibit external stimuli and permit attention to be focused upon important central problems within the child's visual field.

Dissociation

Due to this ever-changing and fragmented picture the child obtains of his environment there is an inability to synthesize experience into meaningful wholes. He tends to respond to things in parts and in segments. There is a close relationship between this factor and distractibility.

Figure-ground Distortions

In various tests administered to the hyperactive child he frequently evidences the inability to pick a figure out of the background, at times he may reverse background and figure, and at other times he may be unable to differentiate between figure and background. Hyperactive children evidence this problem when asked to catch balls thrown at them; their inability to catch well probably stems from initial confusion experienced as they attempt to see the ball against a background.

Perservation

Perservative errors are made frequently by the hyperactive child. He seems unable to "throw-off" the elements of a task previously attempted, and to make new and different responses to one at hand. The consensus of individuals investigating this characteristic in disturbed children indicates that the child is unaware of his preservative errors, and that their presence invariably accompanies other behaviorial disturbances.

Motor Disinhibition

The hyperactive child obeys every impulse to move. He is unable to inhibit his motor activity and responds to every stimuli which encourages movement. He is constantly handling objects, moving his body hither and yon in a classroom and seems to be in perceptual motion from morning to night. While thus engaged, the child may evidence basic neuromotor distrubances seen in the inability to balance well, and in general clumsiness. However, whether the child seems to possess basic movement attributes or is handicapped by movement problems of a mild or severe nature seems no deterrent to actions in which he constantly engages.

Faulty Perception of the Body

The hyperactive child frequently evidences perceptual distortions reflected in various tests of body image. He finds it difficult to name his body parts accurately and to make accurate right-left discriminations, but also may be unable to accurately locate his body relative to objects in response to directions such as "place your left side toward the box." In addition, he is unable to locate objects relative to his body (i.e. "When is the object in front of you, to your left side, to your back, etc.?").

Summary

As is apparent some of these variables are primarily perceptual, others are perceptual-motor and others seem more pure motor (motor disinhibition). There are overlapping areas of malfunction. The total impression such as a child makes upon an observer is that of general disorganization. He seems unable to organize his environment, himself, and the space around him. His movements and speech are inappropriate and rambling, while it is generally accepted that his auditory perception is similarly disorganized. Several basic principles have been advocated when working with such a child within the educational environment. These principles also hold implications for the motor education of such a child. While at the same time the utilization of various activities involving the total body in action may aid in improving his performance in classroom tasks.

Reduce Distractions. It is generally advocated that removal of distractions in the form of extraneous objects, other people, and simply in the amount of space available to the child will lead to learning improvement. As the child is stimulated by everything within his environment, the attempt is made to reduce the number of things to which he can react. In a program of movement education such children should be worked with in small groups with only one thing present (i.e. a mat, or a balance beam).

Carefully Structure the Learning Experience. These children have no tolerance for materials which they perceive as too difficult or too easy. At the same time they are attracted by novelty, but quickly "use up" novel experiences and wish to pass on to other things. This kind of behavior places a responsibility upon the teachers to present materials which are at the optimum level of difficulty and to construct a sequence of materials carefully so that simple and discrete steps are taken from the simple concept to the complex judgment.

Heighten the Attraction of the Task. In addition to the removal of extraneous stimuli, it is frequently suggested the task at hand be made a stimulating experience. Stimulation might be heightened, for example, through the use of vivid colors.

Teach Relaxation. Using relaxation techniques suggested by Jacobson in his 1938 text titled *Progressive Relaxation*, and similar methods, brain-damaged children can be taught to relax. Tactile, verbal, and kinesthetic cues can be given such children as they are placed in a back-lying position which will aid them to better perceive excess tension and to better control general and specific indices of unwanted muscular effort.

Provide Carrells. A most interesting technique is for the teacher to provide booths into which the child may *choose* to go if he feels himself becoming over-stimulated. I have observed this technique in action within recent months in classes for the educationally handicapped in the Los Angeles City Schools. The fact that these children find their hyperactivity unpleasant and seek to correct it *themselves* by placing themselves in such isolation booths would seem to be a helpful step in their educational development.

A PROGRAM FOR KINESIOLOGISTS

A consideration of the above information could lead the kinesiologists toward meaningful research on this problem and/or might suggest helpful clinical procedure which might be employed to aid in the education of individual children. In both cases, it is suggested that the kinesiologist align himself with a clinical psychologist and/or child psychiatrist, as the problems such children present transcend the simple analysis and correction of their observable movement behavior.

A prevalent supposition among educators and physical educators, utilized by some as justification for exercise and physical education, is dependent upon a *drainage theory*. In short, such a theory proposes that vigorous activity of a gross nature serves educational purposes by draining undue tensions, undesirable agressions and hostilities, and other interfering physical-emotional nuances from the child's personality thus leaving his "mind" free to think clearly. Such a theory applied to the hyperactive child might suggest practices which would place him in a situation which would encourage exhausting physical activities, in order to leave him to sedentary classroom activities.

After working with such children in amenable clinical setting during the past several years, and upon consulting some of the recent research, it is believed that the worth of such practices is extremely doubtful. It has been observed that exposure to activities which are unduly vigorous seems only to heighten the child's general irritability, excitability, hostility, and confusions.

Generally it is believed, however, that activities which require gross movement, or a series of movements, are extremely helpful when working with hyperactive children. These experiences must be carefully selected with regard to optimum level of novelty and difficulty, and at the same time be administered initially in settings which are relatively free from distractions. These activities are helpful, of course, in so far as they may improve the physical qualities necessary for their execution. Far more important, however, they present experiences in which the child is rather totally involved, an involvement which is immediately apparent to the teacher-observer—far more apparent than the flicking of the eye across a printed page.

Balance beams gradually lengthened, obstacle courses whose difficulty is increased in discrete steps, and similar activities have been found helpful as devices with which to focus the attention of such children. Their attention span is often measurable (i.e. how long he looks at a balance beam when asked to walk it can not only be clocked with a stopwatch but is also measurable by noting how far he walks before stepping off due to inattention). Recently a child with whom the writer has been working increased the time he focused upon motor tasks from ten seconds to about four minutes. The task in this instance consisted of repeatedly walking the straight edge of a rocking board, and attempting to place his feet into colored footprints.

In addition, the writer has found in his clinical program that verbalization of unilateral activities engaged in by such children aids them to form a heightened sense of the left-right dimensions of their body. Likewise, movements carried out in front of mirrors, or when copying the movements of the instructor also seem to help them to gain a better concept of their body image. Thus motor activities involving the use of the body, perhaps, might serve to partially correct the faulty perceptions the hyperactive child has of himself.

In summary, therefore, it is suggested that motor activities may help to focus the hyperactive child. They serve as experiences which when engaged in, mold behavior so that one can immediately discern whether attention is meaningfully focused. Basically, it is assumed, therefore, that if the hyperactive child's attention can be "captured" through gross motor activities for a period of time greater than the time he has attended to *anything* in the past, his attention span in the classroom may likewise be lengthened. Whether the effects of motoric training are directly reflected in improvement of classroom learning has not been subjected to experimental verification. However, research dealing with this possibility would seem an important undertaking.

To suggest to kinesiologists-physical educators, that they should encourage relative immobility, and that all-out effort is not always desirable, seems to smack of irreligious blasphemy However, in the case of the hyperactive, perceptually disturbed youngster, motor tasks best serve to focus attention rather than simply to make him "fit" or to provide ways of transporting a ball across a field.

REFERENCES

1. Bender, L., and Silver, A.: Body image problems of the brain-damaged child *J Soc Issues,* 4:84, 1948.
2. Cruickshank, William M.; Bentzen, Frances A.; Ratzeburg, Frederick H., and Tannhauser, Mirian T.: *A Teaching Method for Brain-injured and Hyperactive Children.* Syracuse University Special Education and Rehabilitation Monograph Series 6, 1961.
3. Kahn, E., and Cohn, L.H.: Organic driveness, a brain-stem syndrome and an experience. *New Eng J Med, 210:*748, 1934.
4. Sarason, S.B.: *Psychological Problems in Mental Deficiency,* 3rd ed. New York, Harper, 1959.
5. Strauss, A.A., and Kephart, N.C.: *Psychopathology and Education of the Brain-Injured Child.* New York, Grune, 1955, Vol. 2.
6. Strauss, A.A., and Lehtinen, L.D.: *Psychopathology and Education of the Brain-Injured Child.* New York, Grune, 1947.
7. Strauss, A.A., and Werner, H.: Disorders of conceptual thinking in the brain-injured child. *J Nerv Men Dis, 96:*153, 1942.

D. The Mentally Retarded

Chapter 21

THE ROLE OF MOTOR ACTIVITIES IN PROGRAMS FOR MENTALLY RETARDED CHILDREN

CLINICIANS AND EDUCATORS working with retarded children often note that mental impairment is
accompanied by decreased capacity for accurate movement. It is also a frequent observation that retardates
encounter difficulty when attempting to name their body
parts and when trying to make other perceptual judgments
relative to their body. They cannot seem to locate themselves in relation to other objects and are often unable to
make correct left-right discriminations. Reflecting these
observations are several evaluative instruments which
have been used to assess general intellectual functioning
through various measures of body awareness (2,4).

There is also an increasing amount of evidence from
a number of experimental laboratories which points to the
inseparability of perception and motion. For example, the
theories of Werner, Witkin, and K. U. Smith are based
upon data which reflect interactions between visual perception and movement (25,26,21). And while such theories
often do not describe in exact terms methods for use in
programs for retardates, they have nonetheless attracted
the interest of many educators dealing with educationally
handicapped youngsters.

These observations and experimental findings have
led educators in recent years to place perceptual-motor
tasks into the general program of education for retarded
children and youth. Several reasons may be advanced for
their inclusion:

1. Social acceptance and self-acceptance are enhanced

if a child's ability to participate in games, given status by his peers, is improved. A general need for achievement is heightened after successful participation in games.

2. Many initial concepts formed by children and infants are gained through movement experiences. A child whose thought processes are inexact may lack certain developmental underpinnings which involve perceptual-motor behavior. An adequate perception of the body, its various dimensions and parts, may be related to the ability to organize space, to read, to spell, and to write.

3. Certain components of classroom learning may be improved through pupil participation in carefully planned physical activities. Remembering the order of a series of actions of a planned obstacle course, for example, offers the child practice in organizing components of a series of letters when dealing with words. Gross motor activities, if properly apportioned, may aid the hyperactive child to focus attention on various tasks for increasingly longer periods of time.

4. Requesting children to think about and to demonstrate ways in which they might modify the performance of a task and presenting them with opportunities to invent games, represents experiences which should enhance creative thinking and problem-solving ability.

Despite the proliferation of interest in motor activities as educational tools for the retarded, most programs of this nature rest upon theoretical assumptions often unsubstantiated by hard data. The available research evidence often provides rather inexact guides for program content.

Prior to World War II, and in the late 1950's and early 1960's, several investigations dealing with various physical attributes of mentally retarded children were carried out (22). The findings of studies by Hayden, and Francis and Rarick demonstrate that the mentally retarded are from two to four years deficient in muscular strength and endurance when compared to normals (12,10). More comprehensive testing programs utilizing the Sloan revision of the Oseretsky also point to the motoric deficiencies of the retardate, with the less favored subgroup generally identified as composed of children evidencing Down's syndrome. The most marked differences between the normal and retarded child are usually found when balance is assessed, a common clinical test of brain damage (13).

Oliver, and Shotick and Thate have presented findings which suggest that improvement in mental measures may be elicited after participating in programs designed to improve motor ability because of a generalized effect due to an improvement of the child's self-confidence (16,19). Many of these investigations are only exploratory in nature. Corder, for example, found that a twenty-day program elicited significant upward shifts in I.Q.; however, only eight subjects were employed in the experimental group (6).

In general, previous findings indicate that with a decrease in mental age one is likely to obtain higher intercorrelations between I.Q. and motor ability. As might be expected higher correlations are obtained between mental and motor measures when the latter involve a complex series of movements, rather than a simple expression of force, power, and/or endurance.

Almost without exception previous studies have collected data from children classified as *educable mentally retarded* (I.Q. from 50 to 70), rather than with children of poorer mental ability. Only the investigations by Pertejo, and Kugel and Reque, present data on children whose mean I.Q.'s are below 50 (17,14). The California Infant Scale of Motor Development has been employed with some success when evaluating the motor competencies of mongoloids (14).

Most of these previous investigations have utilized too few subjects within various categories upon which to establish valid norms. The findings presented have frequently suffered from a lack of appropriate statistical verification (6,16), while at the same time the battery of tests have been somewhat limited in their scope. Indices of body-image are rarely compared to motor attributes despite the fact that a recent investigation by Guyette, Wapner and others contains findings which suggest that as the retarded child grows older he becomes more dependent upon modifications in bodily tonus when making visual judgements (11).

It is often difficult to adequately survey the abilities of retarded children due to the scarcity of a reasonably large number of children on a single facility. Other difficulties when doing research on these problems arise as one attempts to gather together a control group. It was thus gratifying to me recently to be asked to act as the consultant for a project in which the perceptual-motor attributes of almost two hundred children with learning problems were assessed.°

During the month of June 1966, an advisory committee, composed of individuals interested in motor development, met and sanctioned a project designed to evaluate the perceptual-motor abilities of retarded children. Specifically, this committee decided that the purposes of the initial summer's testing program should be (a) to devise and ascertain the reliability of a test battery; (b) to establish norms from the data collected; and (c) to draw implications from the data relative to programs for the mentally retarded.

In addition, it was decided that an extension of this investigation should involve the assessment of the influence of programs of perceptual-motor education carried out over extended periods of time upon selected attributes of retarded youth.

The battery of tests established, with advice from various members of the advisory committee, was composed of tasks designed to evaluate six attributes: body-perception, gross-agility, locomotor behavior and agility, balance, throwing, and tracking. The scoring system devised permitted two levels of difficulty to be scored. The battery was designed so that it could be administered to a single child within a period of twenty to thirty minutes, in a small room, and would require a minimum of equipment.

°A research project sponsored by the Mental Retardation Services Board of Los Angeles County. Cooperating agencies included the Los Angeles County Department of Parks and Recreation, the Special Education branch of the Los Angeles City Schools, and the Physical Education Department, University of California, Los Angeles (7).

A testing handbook was written, and testers were trained.

During the initial part of the testing program, eighty-three TMR's and EMR's were tested, twice each, at two facilities in order to determine the tests' reliability. During the second phase of the testing program, an additional ninety-four retarded children were tested, one time each, on ten different sites (schools of special education within the Los Angeles City School District).

Norms were established for the various subgroups of subjects by age, and by test. Intertest relationships were surveyed to draw implications for programs for the retarded, and developmental trends were assessed within the data.

Of the subjects, 67 per cent were male, and 24 per cent were Negro. There were no significant differences in any of the scores collected between Negroes and Caucasians, nor between males and females. Forty-six per cent of the subjects were TMR's, with the remainder evenly divided between EMR and educationally handicapped classifications. Twenty-four per cent of the TMR evidenced Down's syndrome. The mean age for the total sample was 11.40 years, with a range of five to twenty-four years.

Analysis of the data revealed the following:

1. The test, and its subtests were reliable, with r's ranging from .74 to .84 when test-retest scores for the subtests were compared, to over .90 when the scores for the total battery were correlated.

2. Age and I.Q. were moderately correlated with the scores in the total battery (.54 and .63 respectively).

3. The mean scores for all the tests taken by the EMR's and EH's were significantly superior to the scores achieved by the TMR's.

4. Most inferior were children classified as evidencing Down's syndrome, primarily in tests evaluating balance.

5. There were higher intertest correlations when the scores of the TMR's were contrasted than when similar measures of the EMR were compared.

6. Most predictive of the total battery score by the

TMR's were their scores on the body-perception category (r=.90). Most predictive of total performance by the EMR's was their score in the balance category (r=.84).

7. The EH's evidenced the poorest crawling and walking patterns; over 90 per cent of the TMR's and EMR's evidenced appropriate cross-extension patterns when crawling and walking.

8. Developmentally, the EMR's and EH's evidenced their best performance during late childhood and early adolescence, with some deterioration noted in their performance means in late adolescence and early adulthood.

9. The mongoloid child evidenced gradual improvement with age in tests evaluating body-perception, agility, and tracking, with no significant improvement noted in tests measuring balance, locomotor agility, and throwing.

10. All subclassifications of subjects evidenced difficulty in making left-right discriminations about their body parts

PROGRAMS FOR THE RETARDED AND EDUCATIONALLY HANDICAPPED

In addition to these general findings, the data collected point to specific applications to programs for various subgroups of retarded and educationally handicapped children. Further research is intended to explore the effect of various kinds of programs upon the attributes evaluated.

Children with Down's Syndrome

It would appear from the data that mongoloid children not only evidence the most severe movement problems, but also their abilities are relatively unaffected as they grow older. At the same time the data indicate that their attributes may change with training, as evidenced by improvements in tasks in which they might have been expected to have practiced (catching a ball). Their most severe problem seems to be balance in tasks indicating an accurate perception of their bodies and in tasks involving movement with visual control (jumping accurately in marked squares).

It would thus seem reasonable that programs for children with Down's syndrome should emphasize activities within these three general areas. Care, however, should be taken to present activities at extremely simple levels to these children. For example, balance training should probably take place initially with the child on "all-fours" as the data indicate that most of these children are unable to balance in an upright position with both knees and feet touching the mat. Training in body-to-object location should be undertaken, for example, by placing a box in a room and asking the child to place his front, back, side, left side, etc. nearest the box.

General agility tasks should also be included in a program for the mongoloids. Their inability to move backwards and to arise efficiently from a lying to a standing position indicates that falling, tumbling, rolling, and other similar movements need considerable practice by this population of children.

Children Who are Trainable Mentally Retarded

In any group of children classified as trainable mentally retarded, one might expect to find from one third to one half who manifest Down's syndrome. Thus the suggestions on the previous pages apply to children within the "trainable" category.

At the same time children who are TMR's and who do not evidence Down's syndrome should be given tasks which lead in a logical way toward activities which are socially acceptable to themselves and to their peers. The decrease in ability indicated in many of the mean scores of this group with increasing age indicates that motivation (or lack of it) proves important as a modifier of performance on the part of the TMR in late childhood or early adolescence.

Thus a perceptual-motor training program for the TMR should include activities designed to enhance balance, body-part perception, body-to-object perception, agility, as well as ball skills, hopscotch, etc. designed to lead into socially approved playground activities.

As is the case with all groups of retarded children, from four to five types of activities within a single forty-five-minute to one-hour training session would seem desirable. If one were to choose the most important activities for the TMR to engage in, they would seem to be practice in body-part perception and in balance. The data indicate that the educator, to be successful, may choose fewer kinds of activities to constitute a program for the TMR than for the EMR. A greater amount of time should be spent with the TMR in practicing these tasks despite the fewer types of activities which would appear to benefit him.

The Educable Mentally Retarded

In contrast to a program for the EMR, the TMR requires a wider variety of activities, and activities which are, of course, more taxing in nature. Their attention span can be expected to be longer than that of the TMR, and they evidence more specific abilities apparently influenced by various kinds of past training to which they have been exposed as individuals.

The single type of activity most important to the total neuromotor development of the EMR appears to be tasks involving balance. Thus tasks involving both dynamic (moving down a balance beam) as well as static posturing would appear to be an important part of a perceptual-motor training program for the EMR.

Additionally, training in left-right discrimination relative to body parts should also be included in such a program. Similarly, training in correct and accurate agility movements involving arm-leg coordination paired with vision should be included. Training in throwing at targets, as well as in correct throwing form should also be included. As the majority of the EMR's could not "place their legs nearest the tester" a portion of an educational program should afford practice in tasks training this important body-to-object attribute. The majority of the EMR's were found unable to accurately cross their body with arm movements and to locate body parts in this manner. This training in lateral arm movements when drawing on blackboards coupled with body-part perception training of a more complex nature should be engaged in by the EMR.

The Educationally Handicapped

This population is being given increased attention by educators throughout the country. Many of these kinds of children are found in classrooms competing unsuccessfully with "normals," and due to rather subtle perceptual-motor impairment have difficulty organizing their bodies, their movements, and components of the visual world.

The data collected on these children revealed a similar *unevenness* which holds important implications for programs designed to enhance their educational abilities. This is one of the few groups in which a relatively large percentage of the members failed to evidence appropriate cross-extension patterns when crawling and walking. Many of these children would probably be classified by the pediatric neurologist as afflicted with slight cerebral palsy or as evidencing other signs of minimal brain damage.

Similar to the other subpopulations surveyed, they evidenced problems when attempting to make left-right discriminations and when asked to cross their body when identifying body parts. At the same time, deficiencies in balance and agility were similarly uncovered. This group of children are frequently beset by emotional problems, as they are usually acutely aware of their perceptual-motor defiencies when they attempt to compete in recreational skills with more skilled children.

These data indicate that programs for such children should include activities designed to enhance skills given status by their peers as well as tasks designed to enhance perception, balance and locomotor agility. It is a common finding that tasks in these latter categories have to be "sold" to the child who is educationally handicapped, as he frequently feels that they are beneath his ability.

The motor skill of EH's is more specific than is evidenced by the TMR's, thus justifying the inclusion of a wider variety of activities for the former group. In summary, activities designed to enhance basic locomotor tasks including crawling, walking, jumping, etc.; activities in body-part perception, balance tasks, together with motor skills which form the basis for culturally desired sports and games, would seem to compose the most meaningful program for the educationally handicapped.

CONCLUSION

It is believed that the kind of research we have described is one of the most fruitful means through which meaningful educational programs for the retardate may be evolved. Such research points to specific practices which appear helpful while delineating others which appear without meaning.

In the not too distant past, arriving at the truth was a relatively simple matter. One only had to listen to and obey the voice of authority. Today the world is more complex. Rational men test their beliefs by reference to the scientific method of problem solving described here today. This newer avenue to the truth results in greater accuracy. Observations are confirmed or disproved through analyses of measurable evidence employing techniques which others can understand and may replicate.

People are complex. Children are complex. Retarded children are complex. To understand the retardate's educational needs, the key is to first attempt to assess each child's unique characteristics. We should attempt to synthesize available knowledge, not ignore it.

REFERENCES

1. Bayley, Nancy: *The California Infant Scale of Motor Development.* Berkeley, U. of Calif., 1936.
2. Benton, Arthur J.: *Right-Left Discrimination and Finger Localization.* New York, Hoeber-Harper, 1959.
3. Benton, Arthur J., and Cohen, B. D.: Right-left discrimination and finger localization in normal and brain-injured subjects. *Proc Iowa Acad Sci, 62*:447, 1955.

4. Berges, J., and Lezine, I.: *The Imitation of Gestures.* London, Spastics Society Medical Education and Information Unit, 1965.
5. Birch, H. G., and Belmont, Lillian: The problem of comparing home rearing vs. foster rearing in defective children. *Pediatrics, 28:*956, 1961.
6. Corder, W. O.: Effects of physical education on the intellectual, physical, and social development of educable mentally retarded boys (unpublished special project). George Peabody College, Nashville, Tennessee, 1965.
7. Cratty, Bryant J. (Project Consultant).: The perceptual-motor attributes of retarded youth (Monogr.). Sponsored by the Mental Retardation Services Board of Los Angeles County Department of Physical Education, 1966.
8. Fallers, S.: An investigation of the motor ability in thirty high grade mentally defective girls with the Oseretsky tests of motor proficiency (unpublished M.A. Thesis). Mac Murray College, 1948.
9. Fait, H. F., and Kupferer, H. J.: A study of two motor achievement tests and their implications in planning physical education acitivities for the mentally retarded. *Amer J Ment Defic, 60*(4):729, 1956.
10. Francis, R. J., and Rarick, G. L.: Motor characteristics of the mentally retarded. U. of Wis., Sept. 16, 1957, U.S. Office of Education Cooperative Research Project No. 152 (6432), 1960.
11. Guyette, Anna; Wapner, Seymour; Werner, Heinz, and Davidson, John: Some aspects of space perception in mental retardants. *Amer J. Ment Defic, 69:*90, 1966.
12. Hayden, F. J.: *Physical Fitness for the Mentally Retarded.* Toronto, Metropolitan Toronto Association for Retarded Children, 1964.
13. Howe, C.: A comparison of motor skills of mentally retarded and normal children. *Except Child, 25*(8):352, 1959.
14. Kugel, R. B., and Reque, D.: A comparison of mongoloid children: JAMA, 175:959, 1961.
15. Malpass, L. F.: Motor proficiency in institutionalized and non-institutionalized retarded children and normal children. *Amer J Ment Defic, 64*(6):1012, 1960.
16. Oliver, J. N.: The effect of physical conditioning exercises and activities on the mental characteristics of educationally sub-normal boys. *Brit J Educ Psychol, 28:*155, 1958.
17. Pertejo, S. J.: La escala metrica de Oseretsky para el examen de motorica (The Oseretsky test for the examination of motor function). *Rev Psicol Gen Apl, 5:*539, 1950, as quoted in *Psychol,* No. 6283, 1952.

18. Rabin, H. M.: The relationship of age, intelligence, and sex to motor proficiency in mental defectives. *Amer J Ment Defic,* 62(3):507, 1957.
19. Shotick, A., and Thate, C.: Reactions of a group of educable mentally handicapped children to a program of physical education. *Except Child,* 26:(5):248, 1960.
20. Sloan, W.: The Lincoln Adaptation of the Oseretsky Test. Lincoln, Illinois, 1948.
21. Smith, Karl U., and Smith, William M.: *Perception and Motion.* Philadelphia, Saunders, 1962.
22. Stedman, Donald J., and Eichorn, Dorothy: A comparison of the growth and development of institutionalized and home reared mongoloids during infancy and early childhood. *Amer J Ment Defic,* 69:391, 401, 1964.
23. Stein, J. U.: Motor function and physical fitness of the mentally retarded: A critical review. *Rehab Lit,* 24(8):230, 1963.
24. Stein, Juliun U., and Rangle, Roy: What research says about psychomotor function of the retarded. *J Health, Rec, Phys Educ, April:*36, 1966.
25. Werner, H., and Wapner, W.: Sensory-tonic field theory of perception. *J Personality,* 18:88, 1949.
26. Witkin, H. A.: Perception of body position and of the position of the visual field. *Psychol Monogr,* 63(7), 1949.

Chapter 22

SOME PERCEPTUAL-MOTOR CHARACTERISTICS
OF CHILDREN AND YOUTH WITH
DOWN'S SYNDROME

S INCE THE EARLIEST descriptions of mongoloids written during the middle of the last century, varying amounts of clinical and experimental attention have been paid to Langdon-Down's "unfinished children." Most frequent are investigations concerned with a microscopic examination of their biochemical and neurological makeup. Such investigations have uncovered evidence in recent years that Down's syndrome is due usually to a trisomy of the twenty-first chromosome. These living mutations are impeded in their functioning by a totality of endocrine, cardiac, and neural deficiencies apparent by the fifth week of fetal development and never evidence physical or mental abilities considered normal.

Relatively few investigations have dealt with some of the more obvious manifestations of their condition—their gross motor attributes. The currently available studies usually classify these children motorically by reference to rather inexact scales of motor development designed to evaluate general maturation levels of normal infants and children (9).

This investigation was promoted by two trends apparent in special education: (a) the increasing awareness on the part of educators that movement experiences constitute one of the most important avenues through which

Speech to California Association for Health, Physical Education, and Recreation, Los Angeles, California, March, 1967.

children with learning difficulties may be educated; and (b) the increase of classes in public schools for the more severely retarded.

Three groups of factors influence the scores on physical ability tests achieved by children with Down's syndrome. Their impaired ability to handle verbal directions, of course, results in lowered scores when any degree of response complexity is required. Mental retardation also seems to reduce their ability to select effective work methods when dealing with motor skills.

Their visual and vestibular mechanisms inhibit their abilities to balance statically and dynamically, qualities underlying most kinds of gross bodily movements.

Additionally, thyroid and pituitary deficiencies result in body builds which are not amenable to strenuous or accurate movement. Their ponderal index (100 times the cube root of body weight divided by stature) is below normal up to about one and one half years, very nearly normal from one and one half to three years, but after that time is significantly above normal. The average mongoloid remains generally obese throughout his lifetime. This writer is unaware of previous investigations which are more than general surveys of general developmental patterns evidenced by mongoloid children.

METHODS AND PROCEDURES

Thirty-eight mongoloid children and youths from the ages of five to twenty-four years were tested individually throughout Los Angeles County during the summer of 1966. These children were evaluated on twelve sites in which they were participating in educational and recreational programs. Their mental ages ranged from "untestable" to I.Q.'s of 50.

The test battery was developed by the writer, consisting of tasks purporting to evaluate six perceptual-motor attributes of retarded children; body-perception, gross ability, balance, locomotor agility, throwing, and tracking-catching. The test consisted of tasks at two levels of difficulty within each of the six categories, and if the child completed the initial level, he was permitted to proceed to the second level. The test was reliable with a test-retest correlation of .91.

FINDINGS

1. Scores obtained from the mongoloids evidence higher intercorrelations than are obtained when similar scores of children with higher intellectual capacities are compared.
2. A correlation of .88 was obtained between the body-perception score and the score in the total battery of tests.
3. The mean scores of mongoloids are in all cases lower than scores obtained from the trainable retardate who does not evidence Down's syndrome. This difference is significant when the total battery scores are compared.
4. Developmentally the balance ability of the mongoloid does not evidence improvement with age. This finding does not, however, imply that training will not improve their balance, as the investigation was not a longitudinal study of change as a function of age.
5. Overall, the mongoloid population with a mean age of approximately ten. years, evidenced perceptual-motor abilities that would be expected in normal children of about three and one-half years.
6. None of the mongoloids evidenced the ability to make any left-right discriminations better than would be expected by chance.
7. The primary problems evidenced by these children were in the performance of tasks in which movement was paired with vision.

It was suggested that movement education programs for these children should emphasize body-perception training, balance tasks, and activities involving agility.

CONCLUSIONS

The severity of the perceptual-motor problems evidenced by the children in this investigation suggested that programs intended to improve these attributes should in- volve tasks designed to improve balance, visual-motor activities of various kinds, and tasks to aid body-part per- ception. Furthermore, it was concluded that mongoloid children, when engaging in perceptual-motor training, should be separated from trainable retardates who do not evidence Down's syndrome.

REFERENCES

1. Bayley, Nancy: *The California Infant Scale of Motor Development.* Berkeley, U. of Calif., 1936.
2. Benda, Clemens E.: *The Child With Mongolism.* New York, Grune, 1960.
3. Crookshank, F.G.: *The Mongol in Our Midst.* New York, Dutton, 1924.
4. Denny, Ray M.: Learning and performances. *Mental Retardation.* Rick Heber and H.A. Stevens (Eds.). Chicago, U. Chicago, 1964.
5. Francis, R. J., and Rarick, G. L.: Motor characteristics of the mentally retarded. U. of Wis., Sept. 16, 1957, U.S. Office of Education, Cooperative Research Project No. 152 (6432), 1960.
6. Kugel, R. B., and Reque, D.: A comparison of mongoloid children. *JAMA, 175:*959, 1961.
7. Pertejo, S.J.: La escala metrica de Oseretsky para el examen de motorica (The Oseretsky test for the examination of motor function). *Rev Psicol Gen Apl,* 5:539, 1950 as quoted in *Psychol,* No. 6283, 1952.
8. Sloan, W.: The Lincoln Adaptation of the Oseretsky Test. Lincoln, Illinois, 1948.
9. Stedman, Donald J., and Eichorn, Dorothy: A comparison of the growth and development of institutionalized and home reared mongoloids during infancy and early childhood. *Amer J Ment Defic, 69:*391, 1964.

E. The Orthopedically Handicapped

Chapter 23

THE USE OF PERCEPTUAL-MOTOR ACTIVITIES FOR ORTHOPEDICALLY HANDICAPPED CHILDREN

INTRODUCTION

THE MORE OBVIOUS problems of an orthopedically handicapped child are frequently accompanied by concomitant psychological and social impairments. His relationships with his peers and parents are often strained. Distortions in social relationships stem from both the manner in which the child perceives his ineptitude, as well as the manner in which various subcultures with which he comes into contact evidence their perceptions of him. The inability to move well may be reflected in various kinds of perceptual distortions involving his body image and/or the ability to organize events in his space field. Distortions in visual-space perception may stem from the lack of opportunity the handicapped child has had to engage in normal manipulatory and exploratory behaviors.

Social Inferiority

The findings of innumerable investigations attest to the fact that orthopedically handicapped children suffer from feelings of social inferiority. These negative feelings are usually more marked in handicapped boys than in girls, perhaps due to the emphasis placed upon successful motoric behavior on the part of males in our society (15).

Speech to the Special Study Institute for Orthopedically Handicapped Children, sponsored by the California State Department of Education, Division of Special Schools and Services, at the Hollywood Roosevelt Hotel, March 21, 1967.

Since there is a strong tendency to judge personality on the basis of physique, some handicapped persons find themselves with less social status, as it is perceived that their "vehicle for action" (their body) is unable to act (23). These kinds of societal reactions result in the tendency on the part of handicapped children to withdraw and/ or to evidence various compensating tendencies, including the excess expression of hostility and aggressions (35). Others with marked physical limitations may engage in equally unrealistic compensations which include ignoring their limitations or other types of overcompensatory behaviors (20).

The normal male child who is accelerated in physical maturity and who evidences the associated physical capacities develops positive and desirable personality characteristics which persist in adulthood. The handicapped child may similarly develop feelings of rejection and inferiority which will tend to persist throughout his lifetime (18).

Problems of social acceptance are often compounded because of the understandable tendency of parents of crippled children to overprotect and/or to reject them (2). The handicapped child's interactions with his family may thus suffer from various kinds of distorting influences. For example, he may be used as a scapegoat in a "game" played between parents who are basically unhappy with each other; or the child may utilize his handicap as a "club" with which to elicit parental favors and/or manipulate parental behaviors (32).

Deprivation of Perceptual-Motor Experiences

Results of the recent evaluations dealing with the effects of early maternal deprivation and intellectual development strongly suggest that a lack of opportunity for movement experiences during the first one or two years of life may result in irreversible sensory-motor and intellectual deficits (10,17). Certain perceptual distortions are evidenced by crippled children. For example, Blane points out that perceived verticality of a rod was in the direction of the affected leg in children who were unilaterally paralyzed; however, the effect seemed more marked in childhood than in adolescence (33). More optimistic findings by Abercrombie and her colleagues, by Dennis, and by Eberhard suggest that the formation of basic concepts may not be dependent solely upon the opportunities the child has to actually move through his environment, but may be gained as the child vicariously engages in manipulating various dynamic situations with which he is confronted by merely watching movement (1,13,14).

The Body Image

Many of the perceptions revolving around the body and its parts are formed by the normally functioning child before his memory is developed. The high correlation we have recently found between body-perception scores and performance on a variety of motor tasks leads us to believe that the formation of this body image is largely dependent upon the child's ability to move effectively; that movement elicits a more accurate concept of the body and that as the growing child gains an awareness of his body and of its position in space, he may then move more effectively (12).

The body image of a child may be evaluated by asking him to point to his body parts or to those of another person in a picture (5). Other assessment devices include asking the child to draw a picture of a child about his own age (1) or to imitate various hand and limb positions performed by the investigator (7). When measures of these kinds are applied to handicapped children, various kinds of developmental gaps and perceptual distortions are evidenced. For example, it has been suggested that the child draws his handicap into most pictures of children he is asked to reproduce.°

Summary

Taking into consideration the findings relative to social interactions, body perception, and visual-space per-

---

° Recent controlled studies, however, indicate that the hypothesized distortion of body image evidenced by handicapped children in draw-a-person tasks was also evidenced by normal children and may be a reflection of every child's inability to draw symmetrical human figures (36).

ception on the part of orthopedically handicapped children, it is apparent that special educational methods are needed to overcome these deficits, just as operations, bracing, and physical therapy are required to ameliorate their more obvious structural problems. It is thus proposed that perceptual-motor activities within three general areas may aid in producing improvement in the psychosocial attributes discussed above. These three areas include training in body-perception, in visual-space perception, and in a type of social-cognitive training through movement which has been termed a "spectrum of styles" (26).

BODY-IMAGE TRAINING

The following sixteen-step sequence was derived from an investigation carried out during the summer of 1966 through the sponsorship of the Mental Retardation Services Board of Los Angeles County. It assumes that the child's body image is formed as the result of a series of dynamic interactions between him and objects and events in his space field. It rejects to some extent the somewhat oversimplified assertion seen in most of the child development literature regarding the fact that first one must help the child to organize his body and then aid him to organize spatial perceptions. The initial sequences involve the organization of the plane surfaces of the body; next, tasks should be utilized which enable the child to gain an awareness of body parts, their movements, and the left-right dimensions of the body. Subsequent to this is the necessity to organize left-right concepts relative to objects in space; next, the left and right of things (using the child's personal reference system); and finally, the projection of the child into others—that other people can have left and right hands, and can move to their left and right, etc.

Activities which should result in the acquisition of these attributes should be comprehensive in scope and utilize tactile movement as well as visual modalities. Body-image training must teach for transfer, and should not consist of favorite tasks which can be counted upon many times only to enhance the ability to perform that particular "game" well.

The steps in this sequence are as follows:
1. Identification of body planes (front, back, side).
2. Body planes in relation to objects (front, back, side).
3. Objects in relation to body planes.
4. Body part identification (limbs, etc.).
5. Movements of the body.
   a. Trunk movement while the body is fixed.
   b. Gross movements in relation to body planes.
   c. Limb and fine movements.
6. Laterality of body.
7. Laterality in relation to objects.
8. Objects related to laterality.
9. Laterality to moving objects.
10. Moving body's laterality to objects.
11. The left and right of objects (personal reference system).
12. Static directionality with other people (projection into another's reference system).
13. Laterality of other people in relation to static objects.
14. Relation of static objects to laterality of other people.
15. Moving objects in relation to others' laterality.
16. Laterality of others' movements.

VISUAL-SPACE PERCEPTION

Orthopedically handicapped children from an early age should be exposed to situations in which they can observe movement. Recent studies have confirmed the fact that even a day-old infant is attracted to objects moving over his crib (16). Specific training techniques can include the introduction of objects on a string to which the child might attend, with the gradual introduction of means whereby he can interact with them through the use of a stick or similar implement. Such devices should be in attractive colors and involve a moderate amount of complexity.

The older child can be exposed to similar experiences and be shown balls swinging in various planes relative to his body. He may simply watch these moving objects, intercept them in various ways, or even catch them if he is able to do so. These moving objects should be varied in size and in speed. More complexity can be introduced into such situations by exposing the child to more than one moving object at a time.

In childhood and adolescence, orthopedically handicapped children should be included in games even if they are merely pushed through relays in their wheel chairs. Such participation not only aids in the formation of desirable social skills, but also presents a series of dynamic movement situations which the child can learn to interpret. Various modifications of standard games are possible and should be participated in as vigorously as possible.

A SPECTRUM OF STYLES

One of the most significant contributions to educational methodology was made in a recent publication by Muska Mosston of Rutgers University (26). In operational terms Mosston has described how one can take a child from a situation in which he is merely reacting to the commands of the teacher to a situation in which he is truly engaging in cognitive behavior. Intermediate to these two stations Mosston interposes teaching-learning situations in which the child is encouraged to interact in purposeful ways with his peers; first as he works with a single student-evaluator, and later as he interacts in a small group.

Situations in which motor activities are utilized offer dynamic confirmation of Mosston's theses which generally revolve around the orderly transfer of decision making from the teacher to the child as the child evidences the ability to assume the responsibility for his own actions. Mosston terms these various styles *teaching by command, teaching by task, reciprocal teaching—the use of the partner, the use of the small group, the individual program, guided discovery, problem solving, and creativity.*

Mosston suggests that each of these steps influences

the child's physical, social, emotional, and intellectual development, with the latter stages in his scheme influencing social-emotional-intellectual functioning to a greater degree.

SUMMARY AND CONCLUSIONS

To enhance the psychosocial attributes of orthopedically handicapped children, three programs involving the use of perceptual-motor activities have been proposed. It is not suggested that these programs are panaceas for the amelioration of all of the mild and severe emotional, perceptual, and social problems of crippled children, but are offered only as techniques to be used in conjunction with the usual methods employed by the psychotherapist, educational counselor, and classroom teacher.

The body-image training program suggests sixteen steps through which the normal child passes from birth to maturity. These steps involve interactions between the child and his environment at several levels, beginning with the identification of the front, back, and sides of the body, and terminating with the tasks enhancing the ability to project oneself "inside" another person's reference system. The program to train visual perception involves the presentation of various dynamic situations to the child. Mosston's Spectrum of Styles was offered as a means through which the socialization process in the handicapped child might be enhanced. The spectrum involves concrete situations through which the child is brought from situations in which he merely reacts to the decisions and commands of another person, to the point where he becomes able to make meaningful and creative decisions for himself

REFERENCES

1. Abercrombie, M. L. J., and Tyson, M. C.: Body image and draw-a-man test in cerebral palsy. *Develop Med Child Neurol*, 8:9, 1966.
2. Allen, F. H., and Pearson, G. H. J.: The emotional problems of the physically handicapped child. *Brit J Med Psychol*, 8: 212, 1928.

3. Barker, Roger G.; Wright, Beatrice A.; Meyerson, Lee, and Gonick, Mollie R.: *Adjustment to Physical Handicap and Illness.* New York, Soc. Sci. Res., 1953.
4. Barsch, R.: Explanations offered by parents and siblings of brain-damaged children. *Except Child,* 27:286, 1961.
5. Benton, Arthur L.: *Right-Left Discrimination and Finger Localization.* New York, Hoeber-Harper, 1959.
6. Benton, Arthur L., and Cohen, B. D.: Right-left discrimination and finger localization in normal and brain-injured subjects. *Proc Iowa Acad Sci,* 62:447, 1955.
7. Berges, J., and Lezine, I.: *The Imitation of Gestures.* Suffolk, Lavenham, 1963.
8. Blane, Howard T.: Space perception among unilaterally paralyzed children and adolescents. *J Exp Psychol,* 63:244, 1963.
9. Boles, G.: Personality factors in mothers of cerebral palsied children. *Genet Psychol Monogr,* 59:159, 1959.
10. Casler, L.: Maternal deprivation: A critical review of the literature. *Monogr Soc Res Child Develop,* 26:2, 1961.
11. Coughlin, Ellen W.: Some parental attitudes toward handicapped children. *The Child,* 6:41, 1941.
12. Cratty, Bryant J.: The perceptual-motor attributes of mentally retarded children and youth (Monogr.). Mental Retardation Services Board of Los Angeles County, August 1966.
13. Dennis, Wayne: Infant development under conditions of restricted practice and of minimum social stimulation. *Genet Psychol Monogr,* 23:143, 1941.
14. Eberhard, Ulrich: Transfer of training related to finger dexterity. *Percept Motor Skills,* 17:274, 1963.
15. Franke, K.: Erforschung der Krüppelpsyche durch selbstdarstellungen gebrechlicher Jugendlichen. *Z Krüppelfursorge,* 25:251, 1932.
16. Haith, Marshall M.: The response of the human newborn to visual movement. *J Exp Child Psychol,* 3:235, 1966.
17. Hunt, J. McV.: *Intelligence and Experience,* New York, Ronald, 1961.
18. Jones, Mary Cover: Psychological correlates of somatic development. *Child Develop* 33:899, 1965.
19. Kammerer, R. C.: An exploratory psychological study of crippled children. *Psychol Rec,* 4:47, 1940.
20. Landis, C., and Bolles, M. Marjorie: *Personality and Sexuality in the Physically Handicapped Woman.* New York, Hoeber, 1942.
21. Leton, Donald A.: Visual-motor capacities and ocular efficiency in reading. *Percept Motor Skills,* 15:407, 1962.
22. Lord, Elizabeth E.: *Children Handicapped by Cerebral Palsy.* New York, Commonwealth Fund, 1937.
23. Lowman, C. L.: Survey of the vocational, educational and social

status of poliomyelitis patients. Conducted for The National Foundation for Infantile Paralysis, 1942 (typescript).

24. Means, Marie H.: Fears of one thousand college women. *J Abnorm Soc Psychol, 31:*291, 1936.

25. Meng, H.: Zur Sozialpsychologie der Korperbeschadigten: Ein Beitrag zum Problem der praktischen Psychohygiene. *Schweiz Arch Neurol Psychiat, 40:*328, 1938.

26. Mosston, Muska: *Teaching Physical Education.* Columbus, Ohio, C. E. Merrill, 1966.

27. Mussen, P. H.: Cripple-stereotypes and attitudes toward cripples (M.A. Thesis). Stanford University, 1943.

28. Mussen, P. H., and Barker, R. G.: Attitudes toward cripples. *J Abnorm Soc Psychol, 39:*351, 1944.

29. Orgel, S. Z., and J. Tuckman: Nicknames of institutional children. *Amer J Orthopsychiat, 1:*61, 1930.

30. Oettinger, K. B.: An experiment in teaching physically handicapped children at home. *Ment Hyg, 22:*245, 1938.

31. Ray, Margaret H.: The effect of crippled appearance on personality judgments (M.A. Thesis). Stanford University, 1946.

32. Ross, Alan O.: *The Exceptional Child in the Family.* New York, Grune, 1964.

33. Schneider, Carl W., and Bartley, S. Howard: A study of the effects of mechanically induced tension of the neck muscles on the perception of verticality. *J Psychol, 54:*245, 1962.

34. White, R. W.: Competence and the psychosexual stages of development. In *Nebraska Symposium on Motivation.* Jones, M. R. (Ed.). Lincoln, U. of Neb., 1960.

35. Winkler, H.: *Psychische Entwicklung und Kruppeltum.* Leipzig, Leopold Voss, 1931.

36. Wysocki, Boleslaw A., and Whitney, Eleanor: Body image of crippled children as seen in draw-a-person test behavior. *Percept Motor Skills, 21:*499, 1965.

APPENDIX

SCREENING TEST FOR EVALUATING THE PERCEPTUAL-MOTOR ATTRIBUTES OF NEUROLOGICALLY HANDICAPPED AND RETARDED CHILDREN

INTRODUCTION

THIS TEST BATTERY has been designed to aid in the identification of children with mild to moderate perceptual-motor problems which may limit their ability to participate in playground games and may to some extent impede their progress in various classroom activities. The battery is divided into two levels with six categories of tests at each level. The tests at the first level are intended to evaluate children with relatively obvious movement problems; the tests at the second level are designed to identify children with mild perceptual-motor impairments.

The selection of tests comprising this battery is based upon the assumption that much of the time perception and movement are inseparable. A child must first accurately judge the pathway a ball is taking as he prepares to catch it. The movements an infant engages in tend to heighten his awareness of his total body and of its parts. Indeed except in the case of reflexive movements, as a hand is quickly withdrawn from a hot stove, most voluntary human actions are heavily "loaded" with perceptual components.

The battery purports to evaluate perceptual-motor functioning involving body perception, gross agility, balance, locomotor agility, throwing skill, and ball tracking

Based upon data from an investigation sponsored by the Mental Retardation Board of Los Angeles County, in cooperation with the Department of Physical Education, University of California, Los Angeles, the Los Angeles County Department of Parks and Recreation, and the Special Services Branch of the Los Angeles City Schools.

skill. Tests in each of these six categories are represented in both levels.

The tests in the sections titled *Body Perception* include tasks designed to evaluate the child's ability to locate himself relative to objects in space, his ability to make left-right discriminations about his body, and the accuracy with which he can identify selected body parts.

The sections in the two parts of the battery dealing with *Gross Agility* involve tasks designed to determine how quickly the child can move his total body with varying degrees of accuracy.

The *Balance* sections on Level I and Level II include tasks intended to evaluate the child's ability to maintain an upright position in space while his method of support undergoes varying amounts of change; with and without visual cues.

The sections titled *Locomotor Agility* contain subtests designed to evaluate how accurately and efficiently the child is able to move his whole body some distance using locomotor activity, including crawling, walking, running, jumping, and hopping.

The sections called *Ball Throwing* contain tests intended to assess the child's ability to accurately and effectively throw a ball. The sections termed *Ball Tracking* are composed primarily of tasks which purport to evaluate the child's ability to anticipate and to react to a moving ball.

The content of the tests which follow have been arrived at empirically, through a survey of the literature, as well as by an analysis of the basic attributes many child development experts view as important to children with perceptual-motor impairments. Initially there has been no attempt to relate these scores to norms which might be achieved by "normal" children of various ages. These tests will be revised and their administration content modified as subsequent data becomes available, and these revisions are proved necessary.

The norms upon which the decile rankings are based were derived from an investigation of over two hundred children carried out during the summer of 1966. The battery is reliable with a correlation of .91 recorded when the test-retest scores of eighty-three children were compared within the same study.

It is believed that most children who can successfully complete all the tests contained in the second level of this battery may be expected to compete effectively with others of their age in moderately difficult playground activities. On the other hand, children who evidence difficulty in these tasks should be limited to participation in programs of basic developmental activities, rather than being exposed to the complexities and frustrations inherent in many of the traditional team games.

Some children, particularly those with slight problems, will evidence an "unevenness" in the manner in which they perform the tasks in the various categories. Some, for example, may be identified who lack specific attributes, i.e. tracking and catching balls. Thus administration of these tests will point to specific curricular implications for certain children or groups of children.

On the other hand, all children should be initially exposed to all the tests on the first level, and if they achieve an overall average of 4.0 (out of a possible 5.0) they should then be given the tests at Level II. If, within a single category in Level I, they score a 5.0, they should be given the tests in the corresponding category at Level II.

TEST ADMINISTRATION

General Information

1. All children should be tested individually in well-lighted rooms approximately 30 by 30 feet in size, with a ceiling about 9 feet in height. There should be no obstructions in the room.

2. Only the tester should be present, and administration time should be about thirty minutes, depending upon whether part or all of the second level is administered.

3. All tests should be described verbally and then demonstarted in exactly the same way the tester wishes the movement to be executed by the child. When it is indicated

in testing directions, the tester may manually assist the desired movement.

4. The tester should follow the directions outlined for the administration of each test as closely as possible. The child should be given every encouragement; and if he asks how he is doing he should be positively reinforced.

5. The initial test administered in Level I should be *Ball Throwing*, in order to gain rapport with the child. With this exception, the tests should be administered in the order given.

6. Each child should be first administered all tests in Level I. If his average score at this level is 4.0 or better, he should be administered the tests in Level II. If any single test in Level I reaches a score of 5.0, he should be given the test in the corresponding category in Level II. Only five points are possible for each test at each level; total ten points per category. Sixty points possible in the total test.

7. When plotting the total score within a single category, the scores from Level I, and Level II should be combined on individual profile sheet.

8. The child should be brought into the room with the tester, introduced, and informed that he will be "playing some games" with the tester for a few minutes." The word *test* should not be used.

Equipment

1. One rubber, air-filled playground ball, dark red in color, 8½ inches in diameter.

2. A solid, white, rubber softball containing a metal cleat so that it can be suspended by a white string. The ball should have a circumference of 12 inches, and the string to it should be 18 inches in length.

3. A foam-plastic, canvas-covered mat, 4 by 6 feet, and 1½ inches thick should be used. This mat should be marked off in 12 one-foot squares, as shown below. Alternate squares should be marked with diagonal lines, as shown, on one side of the mat. In the center of the reverse side of the mat a black oilcloth square 2 by 2 feet should be

placed when the target throw is evaluated. All of the tests except the pattern jumping should be given on this reverse side, and the black target should only be in place when the target throw is administered.

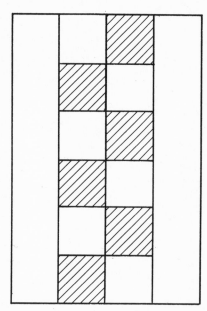

4. A clipboard and scoring sheets.
5. A stopwatch or a watch with a second hand.
6. The mat is Style 806, 4 by 6 feet, costing $2.30 per square foot, solid blue color.°
7. The lines on the mat are made with one-inch, yellow Scotch tape, #471.

TEST ADMINISTRATION—LEVEL I

Level I — Test 1: Body Perception

Equipment: 4 by 6 foot mat.
Preparation: The child should be placed, standing on

°These mats have Valero touch fasteners on the 6 foot edges to permit instant attachment. They have rubberized fabric on their underside to prevent them from sliping. They are made from 1½-inch shock-absorbing polyethylene foam-covered with a tough blue vinyl covering.

the floor, with his toes against the mid-point of the 4-foot edge of the mat. The tester should stand next to the child, with his feet on the floor.

General Considerations: The tester should describe and then demonstrate each movement, and then arise from the mat permitting the child to respond. The child should arise after each request and stand at the starting point described above. The child should be told "thank you" after attempting each movement.

Testing:

a. "_____, please lie down on the mat like this on your front or stomach." (Tester then lies on his stomach, his head away from the child, remains for two seconds, arises, and says, "Now try to do it too." Point is given if the child lies on his stomach regardless of whether or not head is turned away from or toward the tester.

b. "_____, now please lie down on the mat like this on your back." Tester lies down slowly on his back, head away from the child, remains for two seconds, arises and then says, "Now try to do it too."

c. "_____, now please lie down on the mat like this on your front or stomach, with your legs nearest me." Tester assumes lying position, with his legs nearest child, arises and then says, "Now try to do it too." The tester should then go to the far end of the 4 foot side of the mat, and face the child with the mat between them. Point is awarded only if feet are nearest the tester and child is on his stomach.

d. "_____, now please lie down on the mat on your side, like this..." Tester lies down on his left side, feet toward the child, arises, and then says, "Now you try to do it too." Point is awarded no matter which side the child chooses to lie upon, nor where the feet are relative to the tester.

e. The tester should then say, "Now let me see you lie down on your left side." This should *not* be demonstrated. A 5th point is awarded in this category if the child correctly lies on his left side.

Scoring: One point is given for correctly executing

each of the requests. No points are deducted for a slowly executed response. Total of five points possible.

Level I — Test 2: Gross Agility

Equipment: 4 by 6 foot mat; stopwatch.

Preparation: Child is asked to stand in the center of the mat facing a 4 foot side and the tester. Tester should be ten feet away. Then the child should be asked to lie down in the middle of the mat, his feet toward the tester.

Instructions: After the child is in the above position, the tester should say, "I would like to see how fast you can stand up and face me." A stopwatch should be started as the child's head leaves the mat, and stopped as he has his knees straight as he assumes a standing position, facing the tester. If the child does not understand; the tester should demonstrate standing up rapidly.

Scoring: 1 point if the child turns to his stomach first and then arises in more than 3 seconds.

2 points if the child turns to his stomach first and arises under three seconds.

3 points if the child sits up without turning over, and stands up without turning his back to the tester, but taking more than three seconds.

4 points if the child sits up, remains facing the tester when arising, and does so in two seconds.

5 points if the child sits up, remains facing the tester when arising, and does so under two seconds.

Note: A second hand on the standard watch may be used in lieu of a stopwatch. Maximum of five points possible.

Level I — Test 3: Balance

Equipment: Stopwatch.

Preparation: The tester should face the child on a level floor ten feet away.

Instructions: After getting the child in this position the tester should say, "I would like to see how long you can stand on one foot like this." The tester should demonstrate balancing on his left foot, using his arms to assist him and should then say, "Now you try it too." Tester should demonstrate the held position for ten seconds.

Scoring: 1 point if attempted and held for 1 second.
2 points if attempted and held from 2 to 4 seconds.
3 points if attempted and held from 4 to 6 seconds.
4 points if attempted and held over 6 seconds.

Second part: "Now let's see if you can balance on one foot with your arms folded, like this." Tester should demonstrate by posturing on one foot with arms folded across his chest for ten seconds.

Scoring: Five points in this test if arm-folded balance is held from three to four seconds. Maximum of five points possible.

Permit the child to remain balanced on both parts of this test for ten seconds, and then suggest that he stop. The scoring is not influenced by the foot he decides to balance upon; however, it should be the same foot throughout.

Level I — Test 4: Locomotor Agility

Equipment: 4 by 6 foot mat.

Preparation: Ask the child to stand on the floor, with his feet touching the mat in the middle of one of its 4-foot sides. The tester should place himself at the same end.

Instructions: After the child is in place, the tester says,

a. "_____, let's see if you can crawl across the mat like this," Tester crawls on hands and knees in the correct pattern down the length of the mat away from the child, then toward the child, and then the tester says, "Now you try it too." One point scored if a correct cross-extension pattern is seen in the crawling movement.

b. "_____, let's see now if you can walk down the mat like this." Tester walks down the mat away from the child and then says, "Now let's see if you can do it too."

Additional point is scored if cross-extension pattern is seen in gait.

c. "_____, now can you jump across the mat like this?" Tester takes three to four jumps across the mat, using both feet together and proper arm lift as he travels and then says, "Now you try too." One point is scored if the child leaves the ground two to three times during trip down the mat.

d. "_____, now let's see you jump backwards down the mat like this." Tester jumps backwards toward the child and then says, "Now let me see you do it." A point is given if the child can jump backwards two to three times without falling down, proceeding down the mat. He is permitted to look behind himself when executing this test. Tester should return to the far end of the mat and await the child, stop him and prevent him from falling on the floor as he completes his trip.

e. "_____, now let's see you hop down the mat on one foot like this." Tester demonstrates one foot hopping, using his left foot across the mat away from the child and then says, "Now let me see you do it." One additional point is scored if child is able to hop on one foot (either one) from two to three times down the mat.

Maximum of five points possible.

Level I — Test 5: Ball Throwing

Equipment: Rubber playground ball, 8 inches in diameter.

Preparation: Ball is placed at the child's feet, tester faces the child, fifteen feet away.

Testing: The child is asked to pick up the ball and throw it to the tester. The tester should say, "_____, please pick up the ball and throw it to me." The tester should then execute a proper one-handed overhand throwing movement. And at the same time he should say, "Like this." The ball is rolled back to the child, and he should be permitted five throws.

Scoring: 1 point is given if he pushes the ball with his hands or feet.

2 points are given if he throws the ball,

either overhand or underhand, using both
arms at the same time.

3 points are given if the ball is thrown with
one arm without any body shift into the throw.

4 points are given if the child throws with a
weight shift forward of the body, without
proper step on the opposite foot.

5 points are given if the child throws with a
weight shift at the time the ball is released,
and with a step with the opposite foot occurring at the same time.

Give the child the proper score based upon the habital
way he selected to throw the ball, i.e. the manner in which
he throws it three out of five times. Maximum of five
points possible.

Level I — Test 6: Ball Tracking

Equipment: 8½ rubber, air-filled playground ball.

Preparation: The child should face the tester ten feet
away. The tester should hold the ball.

Testing: The tester should then say, "Now I will
bounce the ball to you; try to catch it any way you can."
The tester then throws the ball so that it bounces once before the child gets it; the ball should bounce so that it comes
chest high to the child. Two practice bounces are permitted
to allow the child and tester to become oriented to the
problem. The tester should then say "Now do you understand? Catch it any way you can, with one or two hands."

Five throws should then be made to the child, bounc-
ing the ball once. The ball may be returned by the child
any way he sees fit. About five seconds should be permitted
between throws.

Scoring: Score one point for each time the ball is
caught and controlled by the child. Maximum of five points
possible.

TEST ADMINISTRATION—LEVEL II

Level II — Test I: Body Perception

Equipment: 4 by 6 foot mat.

Preparation: The child is asked to lie on his back in the center of the mat, with his feet pointed toward the 4-foot end; the tester should stand at this end.

Testing: The tester should say, "_____, now I am going to ask you to do certain tahings with your arms and legs; please try to do them as quickly and as accurately as you can. First close your eyes." Then the tester should say,

1. "Raise your left arm in the air." Then the tester should wait until the child makes a decision and moves. Then the tester says, "Put your arm down now."

2. The tester should then say, "Raise your left leg up." The tester should wait until the leg is decided upon and moved and then say, "Put your leg down now."

3. The tester should then say, "Raise you right arm in the air." The tester should wait until the child selects an arm and raises it and should then say, "Put your arm down now."

4. The tester should then say, "Touch your left elbow with your right." After some movement is made, the tester should say, "Now bring your hand down again."

5. The tester should then say, "Touch your right knee with your left hand." After these movements are completed, the tester should ask the child to open his eyes and come to his feet.

Scoring: One point is awarded for each correctly executed movement. No points are deducted for slowly executed movements. If in numbers one through five, the movements are correct, but with wrong hand in every case, i.e. all movements backwards, a total of three points is awarded to the child for this test. Maximum of five points possible.

Level II — Test 2: Gross Agility

Equipment: 4 by 6 foot mat.

Preparation: Child is placed in the center of the mat, standing and facing one of the six-foot edges. The tester stands ten feet away facing the child.

Testing: "_____, see if you can kneel down on one knee at a time, and then stand up on one leg at a time like this without touching anything." The tester then executes a four count, one to the second, movement kneeling first on one knee, then on the second, then standing on the first foot and arising on two feet. The tester says then, "Do you understand?" "Would you like to see it again?" If the child wishes to see the movement again, the tester should do so; after this second demonstration, the tester should then say, "Now you try it too."

> *Scoring:* 1 point is awarded if the child uses his hands on his thighs *and* on the floor to assist him in descending and/or arising.
>
> 2 points are awarded if the child touches one or both hands to his thighs when ascending and descending, or if the child comes down to both knees at once, or gets to both feet at the same time.
>
> 3 points are awarded if the child uses one or both hands only while getting up or if he falls to one knee while arising.
>
> 4 points are awarded if the child executes movement without the use of the hands, but there is general unsteadiness, i.e. extra steps taken as the child resumes his feet, etc.
>
> 5 points are awarded if the child executes movement perfectly with the hands at the sides, not assisting the movement, and with the feet coming down and up separately.
>
> No points are deducted if the child comes up first with a different foot from the one kneeled upon. Maximum of five points possible.

Level II — Test 3: Balance

Equipment: Stopwatch.

Preparation: Place the child in the standing position on a level floor and facing away from obstacles, with the tester ten feet away.

Testing: After placing the subject in the position described above, the tester should say,

a. "I would like to see if you can stand on one foot like this (the tester should fold his arms) with your arms folded for ten seconds."

b. If the child can accomplish this for five seconds or more, the tester should say, "I would now like you to balance on one foot like this, with your arms at your sides and your eyes closed."

c. If the child can accomplish this for five seconds or more, the tester should say, "I would like you to balance on one foot with your eyes closed and your arms folded like this." The tester should demonstrate with eyes closed, an arm-folded, one-foot balance.

d. If the child can accomplish this for five seconds, the tester should say, "Now try to balance on one foot with your eyes closed, arms held at your sides, but using the other foot this time" The tester should be aware of the foot preferred by the child and request that the opposite one be used.

e. If the child can accomplish this for five seconds, the tester should say, "Now try to balance on the same foot (non-preferred) with your arms folded and your eyes closed."

Scoring: One point is scored for each of the above tests completed successfully, i.e. held over five seconds. No points are given if the arms become unfolded if they are required to be folded, or if the child opens his eyes when they are required to be closed.

In each case the stopwatch should be started, or the second hand observed, as the foot leaves the ground and stopped when it touches the next time. "Arms at your sides," means that the child can use the arms for maintaining his balance in any way that is helpful.

From ten to fifteen seconds rest should be permitted between trials. Maximum of five points possible.

Level II — Test 4: Locomotor Agility

Equipment: 4 by 6 foot mat laid out in 12 one-foot squares.

Preparation: The child should face the tester at the

far end of the middle of a 4-foot side. The tester should stand on the floor with his feet at the middle of the other end of the 4-foot side of the mat, facing the child.

Testing: With the child and tester in the above positions, the tester should say,

a. "Now let's see if you can jump down the mat like this." The tester then jumps two feet at a time down the mat, moving straight ahead, and jumping carefully in all six squares. The tester should then say, "Now let's see you do it; be sure to jump in each square and move straight ahead."

b. After this is attempted, the tester should say, "Now let's see you jump back and forth (using only the unmarked squares so that he jumps forward with each jump) like this." The tester should then say, "Now let's see you do it; be sure to jump only in the unmarked squares."

c. After this is attempted, the tester should say, "Now let's see you jump backwards down the mat like this." The tester should jump directly backwards down the mat, using both feet, and landing in all six squares. The tester should then say, "Now let's see you do it too; be sure to jump in all six squares." The child can be permitted to look backwards as he jumps.

d. After this is attempted, the tester should say, "Now let's see you hop down the mat like this." The tester should then hop on the mat straight ahead, using all six squares. The tester should then say, "Now let's see you do it. Jump in each square and move straight ahead."

e. After this is attempted, the tester should say, "Now let's see you hop down the mat like this." The tester should then hop on one foot, hopping only in the unmarked squares, so that every hop moves him forward and from side to side. The tester should then say, "Now let's see you do it too; be sure only to hop in the unmarked squares."

Scoring: One point is given for each successful trip, i.e. one with less than two errors in it. An error is scored when a foot (or feet) does not land in a square, when the second foot is touched when hopping on one foot, or when an extra step is taken in a square. Maximum of five points possible.

Ten to fifteen seconds rest should be permitted between trips. Either foot may be used for hopping, but the same foot must be used for each trip.

Level II — Test 5: Ball Throwing

Equipment: Playground ball 8½ inches in diameter. 4 by 6 foot mat with target side up.

Preparation: The child should stand fifteen feet away from the 4-foot end of the mat.

Testing: After the child has assumed the above position, the tester should stand next to him and throw the ball toward the mat's center on which is painted a 2 by 2 foot square "target." This should be done three times, and the tester should then say, "I would like you to take this ball and try to make it drop in the center of the mat. Do you understand?"

If the child is aware of the nature of the task, he is permitted to throw, either overhand or underhand, with one or two hands, at the target five times.

Scoring: 1 point is given if three attempts have hit the mat, but not the center target.

2 points are given if five attempts have hit the mat, but not the target.

3 points are given if two attempts have hit the target regardless where other throws have landed.

4 points are given if three attempts have hit the target, regardless where other throws have landed.

5 points are given if four or five throws land within the target.

The child receives one of the scores above; highest score possible is five points.

Level II — Test 6: Ball Tracking

Preparation: The tester should face the child about two feet away; he should ask the child to extend his arm at the shoulder, fist clenched. He should then suspend the ball on the 15-inch string so that it hangs, when motionless at the level of the child's chin (top of the ball just under the chin) and a distance away determined by the length of the child's arm plus the clenched fist.

The ball should then be suspended by the tester's left hand so that it hangs as described above. The ball should then be grasped with the tester's right hand, brought to a position which makes the string horizontal, and released so that it swings from the child's left to right in a vertical plane, parallel to the one in which the child is standing.

Testing: The tester should then permit the ball to swing back and forth in this manner six times and ask the child to watch it. The tester should then say, "See this ball swing back and forth? See if you can touch it with one finger like this (the tester holds the ball motionless with one hand and uses the opposite index finger on the ball touching it quickly with the tip of the opposite index finger) as it passes by you."

The tester should then hang the ball in front of the child and make sure that he starts his movement from his side, and that the touch is made directly in front of the child.

The tester should start the ball five times, allowing it to swing past the child three times after each release. As soon as the child touches it or attempts to, or the hand is extended and the ball comes back on it, and stops, the ball is stopped by the tester and started again.

Scoring: Score one point (maximum five) for each time during each of the five sets of three swings each that the child is able to touch the ball. Make sure that no score is given if the ball touches the hand, i.e. as it swings back to the extended hand after a "miss" has occurred.

(Examiner)

(Adm. No.)   (Subject No.)

SCORE SHEET

(Date)   (Name)   (Age)   (Sex)

Motor Problems?————, Diagnosed as ————————————————————————————
              (yes-no)

Degree of Retardation ——————————————————————— I.Q.————————

SCORES   LEVEL I   LEVEL II

Test 1: Body Perception   Body Perception

a. stomach-front ———————————   a. left arm   ———————————
b. back   ———————————   b. left leg   ———————————
c. stomach-legs ———————————   c. right arm ———————————
d. nearest tester   d. left elbow
   side   ———————————   e. left knee ———————————
e. left-side   ———————————

   Total Score   ———————————   Total Score ———————————

Test 2: Gross Agility (quick get-up)   Gross Agility (kneel and rise)

   Total Points ———————————   Total Points ———————————

Test 3: Balance (eyes open)   Balance (arms folded, eyes closed)

   Total Points ———————————   Total Points ———————————

Test 4: Locomotor Agility (crawl-hop)   Locomotor Agility (pattern jump-hop)

   Total Points ———————————   Total Points ———————————

Test 5: Ball Throwing (form)   Ball Throwing (at target)

   Total Points ———————————   Total Points ———————————

Test 6: Ball Tracking (swinging ball)   Ball Tracking (catching)

   Total Points ———————————   Total Points ———————————

Total Points in Battery: Level I ————— Level II —————————

Average score Level I   ——————— Average Score Level II ———————————

                    Total Score, Total Battery

                    Average Score, Total Battery ———————

DECILE RANKINGS OF SCORES IN THE TOTAL BATTERY FOR THE CHILDREN WITH DOWN'S SYNDROME, CLASSIFIED BY AGE

Decile	Age				
	5-8 Yrs	9-12 Yrs	13-14 Yrs	15-18 Yrs	19-22 Yrs
1	20+	25+	23+	40+	30+
2	18-19	24-22	21-22	37-39	28-29
3	17	20-21	19-20	32-36	26-27
4	15-16	18-19	18	28-31	24-25
5	13-14	15-17	16-17	25-27	22-23
6	11-12	13-14	14-15	19-24	20-21
7	10	11-12	13	15-18	18-19
8	9-8	9-10	11-12	11-14	17-16
9	7	6-8	9-10	6-10	14-15
10	6-	5-	7-	5-	13-
	M=13.95 SD=4.79	M=15.46 SD=6.71	M=16.23 SD=5.00	M=21.11 SD=13.03	M=21.76 SD=5.39

Locate the child's raw score in the proper age column. Decile ranking indicated in left hand column indicates approximate placement of the child's score in the total population surveyed in this investigation, i.e. a child with a decile ranking of "3" has achieved a score on the total battery which is better than 70 per cent of other children his same age and mental level.

DECILE RANKINGS OF SCORES IN THE TOTAL BATTERY FOR THE
TMR's, CLASSIFIED BY AGE

Decile   *Age*

Decile	5-6 Yrs	7-8 Yrs	9-10 Yrs	11-13 Yrs.	14-16 Yrs.	17-20 Yrs	21-24 Yrs
10	28+	32+	47+	31+	41+	46+	48+
9	24-27	27-31	32-46	26-30	35-40	42-45	43-47
8	21-23	23-26	28-31	24-25	34-30	41-35	39-42
7	18-20	20-22	25-27	20-23	26-29	36-37	35-38
6	15-17	17-19	22-24	17-19	22-25	33-35	22-34
5	12-14	13-16	18-21	14-16	17-21	30-32	28-31
4	9-11	10-12	14-17	11-13	13-16	27-29	25-27
3	6-8	6-9	11-13	7-10	9-12	23-26	21-24
2	2-5	1-5	5-10	3-6	2-8	19-22	15-20
1	1-	0	4-	5-	2-	18-	
	M=14.42 SD=10.06	M=15.96 SD=11.88	M=20.65 SD=11.93	M=16.30 SD=13.78	M=21.20 SD=10.28	M=32.12 SD=10.28	M=31.10 SD=12.58

Locate the child's raw score in the proper age column. Decile ranking indicated in left hand column indicates approximate placement of the child's score in the total population surveyed in this investigation, i.e. child with a decile ranking of "3" has achieved a score on the total battery which is better than 70 per cent of other children his same age and mental level.

DECILE RANKINGS OF RAW SCORES IN THE
TOTAL BATTERY FOR THE EMR'S

Decile	*Age*			
	5-8 Yrs	9-10 Yrs	11-14 Yrs	15-20 Yrs
1	56+	47+	54+	45+
2	48-55	45-46	50-53	41-44
3	41-47	43-44	47-49	38-40
4	36-40	41-42	45-46	36-37
5	30-35	39-40	43-44	34-35
6	34-21	36-38	40-42	31-33
7	20-30	34-35	37-39	28-30
8	13-19	32-33	35-36	25-27
9	4-12	30-31	31-34	22-24
10	3-	29-	30-	21-
	M=30.03 SD=19.85	M=38.19 SD=6.82	M=41.95 SD=8.53	M=32.95 SD=8.80

Locate the child's raw score in the proper age column. Decile ranking indicated in left hand column indicates approximate placement of the child's score in the total population surveyed in this investigation, i.e. a child with a decile ranking of "3" has achieved a score on the total battery which is better than 70 per cent of other children his same age and mental level.

DECILE RANKINGS OF SCORES IN THE TOTAL BATTERY FOR THE EH'S, CLASSIFIED BY AGE

Decile	Age			
	5-8 Yrs	9-10 Yrs	11-12 Yrs	13-16 Yrs
1	23+	57+	60	60
2	20-22	54-56	60	55-59
3	17-19	50-53	58-59	51-54
4	15-16	46-49	54-57	49-50
5	14-	43-45	50-53	45-48
6	13-	40-42	45-49	42-44
7	11-12	37-39	40-44	40-41
8	8-10	34-36	35-39	37-39
9	5-7	30-33	27-34	34-37
10	4-	29-	33-	33-
	$M = 13.95$ $SD = 6.71$	$M = 41.95$ $SD = 9.18$	$M = 48.84$ $SD = 16.83$	$M = 44.23$ $SD = 8.14$

Locate the child's raw score in the proper age column. Decile ranking indicated in left hand column indicates approximate placement of the child's score in the total population surveyed in this investigation, i.e. a child with a decile ranking of "3" has achieved a score on the total battery which is better than 70 per cent of other children his same age and mental level.

INDIVIDUAL PROFILE SHEET

(Child's Name) _____

C.A. _____ (Tester) _____ Sex _____ Height _____ (Date) _____ Weight _____ (Location) _____

	Body Perception	Gross Agility	Balance	Locomotor Agility	Throwing	Tracking	
10	0	0	0	0	0	0	0
9	0	0	0	0	0	0	1
8	0	0	0	0	0	0	2
7	0	0	0	0	0	0	3
6	0	0	0	0	0	0	4
5	0	0	0	0	0	0	5
4	0	0	0	0	0	0	1
3	0	0	0	0	0	0	2
2	0	0	0	0	0	0	3
1	0	0	0	0	0	0	4
	0	0	0	0	0	0	5

Average Per Test Category _____

Total Battery Score _____

Remarks: _____

A MOBILITY ORIENTATION TEST FOR THE BLIND

T HE TWO COMPONENTS of this test were developed following the completion of an investigation titled The Perceptual Thresholds of Non-Visual Locomotion, carried out under a grant from the Public Health Service (NB 05577-02S1.

The survey of the findings suggested that two assessments might aid peripatologists to identify some of the basic perceptual attributes of the blind. With this in mind, two simple procedures were developed based upon the normative data collected in this investigation. One of these was developed to evaluate the veering tendency, the expected accuracy limits when attempting to walk a straight course without vision. The second was devised to evaluate the perception of gradient. Thus, the first one should determine how accurately persons can perceive their direction when attempting to walk a straight pathway in a horizontal plane, while the second attempts to determine the accuracy with which an individual can judge the shape of a pathway walked in a vertical plane. These tasks are presented as only two of several possible evaluative procedures which might be utilized prior to and at the completion of mobility training program. Additional ones will be added to these, and the administration and the scoring of these two will be modified when additional data become available.

Several criteria governed the selection and administration of these two tests: (a) The expense of their administration is kept to a minimum; (b) Only perceptions relative to locomotion are surveyed; (c) Measurement

Data were processed at the Health Sciences Computing Facility, Medical Center, UCLA.

procedures are simplified; (d) A minimum of equipment time, area, and apparatus is needed.

EVALUATION OF THE VEERING TENDENCY

The data for the tests evaluating the veering tendency were obtained from four groups of blind subjects: twenty children, six to eleven years of age; forty adolescents, thirteen to nineteen years of age; seventy-eight adults, twenty to fifty-nine years of age; and thirty-three aged, fifty-nine years of age and older. The norms for adolescence were not separated by sex; although marked differences relative to the average amount of angular rotation per hundred feet of pathway walked were found between male and female adolescents, these sex differences were not significant upon contrasting deviation at 100 feet. In order to limit the area necessary to administer this test, norms for only 100 feet of forward movement were employed, following an initial 50 feet in which the subject establishes his subjective feelings of "straightness." The deviation between groups *at* 100 feet did not always correspond to the average amount of veer evidenced *per* hundred feet. For example, the adolescents were the most accurate movers when the angular rotation for their entire three hundred foot pathway was computed; however, they were the most inaccurate group when measuring their *deviation in feet at 100 feet.*

The test for veering tendency was based on the following assumptions: (a) It is helpful to know, relative to another of comparable age, whether an individual evidences a marked or a slight tendency to veer; the breakdown utilized in this test is *good, fair,* and *poor;* (b) Independent of auditory cues available, the blind are safer and can move more accurately in the average neighborhood, composed of sidewalks and streets which are relatively straight, if they are able to walk a straight pathway from 50 to 150 feet.

The deviation in feet at 100 feet is computed from graphs drawn which were based upon both the average angular rotation measured at 100, 200, and 300 feet, as well as upon the mean deviation at 100 feet from the initial center line (based upon the mean deviation on the *y* axis of the graphs originally utilized to collect the data). The *good* area on the graphs thus represents one standard deviation; one half of a standard deviation to the right and one half to the left of the initial straight line. The *fair* areas are an additional one half of a standard deviation to the left and to the right of the *good* area; while the *poor* areas on the graphs represent additional one-half standard deviations to the left and to the right of the *fair* area.

Test Administration

A line 150 feet long should be drawn on a level grass field with lines marked in feet drawn at right angles to this line at the 50-foot mark and at the end of the line (at the 150-foot mark). These cross lines should be marked in one-foot intervals; at the 50-foot mark the line should be 50 feet long (25 feet on either side of the initial straight line) and the line 200 feet long should be drawn across the end of the 150-foot line. Care should be taken to mark the lines without indenting the surface of the field. If a cement area is utilized, it is to be expected that the subjects will be more accurate than on the grass field (Fig. 1).

The subjects should first be informed that they will be asked to continue to walk a straight line after being guided for five steps initially. They should then be deprived of auditory cues via the insertion of rubber ear plugs and cotton. Secondly, visual cues should be eliminated by opaque masks and/or blindfolds. Finally, opaque cloth hoods should be placed over their heads and shoulder to eliminate shadows, light, and wind cues. They should then be led to the starting point at the beginning of the 150-foot line that is crossed by the two lines marked in feet at 50 and 150 feet. They should be guided from behind at the elbows for five steps and then released, taking care not to do this in an abrupt manner which might disorient them. The tester should then follow and mark on a similar smaller pattern, placed on a clipboard, the deviation, in feet, at 50 feet and at 150 feet of forward motion based upon the points on the cross lines touched by the subjects as they walk. The most valid measure of the veering tendency, it is believed, will be obtained on the first trial. The amount of veer evidenced on the second and subsequent trials is influenced, to a large degree, by the manner in which the testee is returned to the starting point and by other cues received relative to the shape of the pattern walked on the first trial. If the subject is led directly back to the starting point over the shortest possible route or over the pathway he has transcribed in the reverse direction, it is to be expected that on the second trial he will deviate less from the initial straight line at 150 feet than on the first trial.

The score of *good, fair,* or *poor* is computed by subtracting the amount of deviation from the initial straight line noted at 50 feet of forward progress from the deviation evidenced at 150 feet, and from comparing the figure arrived at to the chart appropriately corresponding to the testee's age.

For example, if an adult of fifty-five years of age deviated 12 feet to the left at 50 feet and 29 feet to the left at 150 feet, his score would be 17 feet. He would thus have received a score of *good* (Figs. 2 to 5).

If the testee deviates at 50 feet in a direction opposite to that deviated in at 150 feet, i.e. crossed the initial straight line after traveling forward 50 feet, the tester should add the deviation at 50 feet to the deviation at 150 feet. For example, if the testee veers 4 feet to the right at the 50-foot mark and then crosses the initial straight line and veers 23 feet to the left by the time the 150-foot mark is reached, his score is 4 plus 23, or 27 feet of deviation.

If the testee crosses the initial straight line more than once between the starting point and the 150-foot mark, only the deviation at the 150-foot mark should be used to compute the score. Utilizing this scoring method, the testee thus establishes his subjective perceptions of a straight pathway during the first 50 feet of travel. The veering tendency score arrived at, thus, is the difference between the deviation at 50 feet and the deviation at 150 feet, so that the final measure constitutes the amount of veer evidenced between 50 and 150 feet. It is, thus, a conservative measure of the actual deviation from the line upon which the testee is initially started.

THE SENSITIVITY TO GRADIENT

The equipment needed to evaluate the sensitivity to decline and incline without vision is as follows: one riser 4 by 8 feet long by at least 1 foot high made of ¾ of an inch of reinforced plywood so that the surface, 4 by 8 feet, may be walked upon without any sag. The riser should have a standard ½-inch thick carpet mat on its 4 by 8 foot side so that foot falls may be muffled. Leading off from each of the 4-feet wide ends of this riser and two adjustable ramps, also four feet wide, whose distal ends may be adjusted in height to produce inclines and declines of 1, 2, 4, and 6 degrees.

After being blindfolded and ear-plugged as in the first test, the subject should be started on one end of the level riser facing one of the ramps; it makes no difference whether the ramp he faces is initially inclined at 1 degree or declined at 1 degree. The subject should then be informed that he is starting on a level riser and then asked to walk and to continually report whether the pathway feels as if it is level, going downhill, or going uphill. As the subject walks, he should be guided at his elbow by the tester. With practice this may be accomplished without the tester's giving a cue as to the gradient walked. Initially, one ramp should be fixed so that it produces a decline of 1 degree, while the other should be fixed to an angle of 1 degree of incline. The testee should be guided when stepping upon one of the four-feet wide ends of the level center riser. Again he should be informed that he is starting on a level pathway and then should be guided across the level riser and onto the ramp which is now inclined (or declined) 1 degree (or 6 degrees) so that he walks a total of about 16 feet. After his report is noted, or no report is forthcoming, the testee should be guided when stepping off the apparatus and then led to the near end of the level riser so that he now faces the ramp which has not yet been traversed and which is placed at a gradient opposite to that of the initial ramp walked. Again he should be guided across the level riser and across the ramp at the opposite end, his reports noted, and then guided when stepping down from the end of the ramp. The first ramp's angle should be changed from 1 degree to 2 degrees, or the angle decreased from 6 degrees to 4 degrees, depending upon whether the initial angle was 1 or 6 degrees. These procedures are continued until the subject reports both incline and decline, if the gradients had been gradually increased, or *stops* reporting sensitivity to incline and decline, if the angles of gradient were progressively decreased. It makes no difference whether the ramps are first set at six degrees and then moved to 4 degrees, etc.; whether the gradient is varied in the opposite direction; or whether the subject first walks over a decline or incline. These procedures should be carried out slowly and deliberately, affording the testee maximum security and permitting him to sit and rest while the gradient changes are made.

The angles of the ramps should not be changed randomly, but in a regular progression, either increasing or decreasing the gradient. One ramp should be employed to evaluate sensitivity to decline and the other to evaluate sensitivity to incline. The score obtained is thus either the angle the testee *first* reports if incline and decline (uphill and downhill) are gradually increased from 1 to 6 degrees; or the angle *last* reported, if the angles of the end ramps are initially set at 6 degrees and then reduced through 4 degrees, 2 degrees, and 1 degree.

As the data did not indicate marked group differences in the perception of gradient, the norms are not classified by age, sex, etc. The following scoring system should be a guideline:

Report on Declines
Sensitive to: $1°$ - good
$2°$ - fair
$4°$ - poor
$6°$ - extremely poor

Report on Inclines
Sensitive to: 1° - excellent
           2° - good
           4° - fair
           6° - poor

If testees are found who are sensitive to 6 degrees of gradient (incline and/or decline) and not to 4, 2 or 1 degrees, it should be expected that they will also evidence marked veering tendencies. It should be also expected that about 50 per cent of the blind testees will report sensitivity to 1 degree of decline, and about 50 per cent will report sensitivity to two degrees of incline.

These two evaluative procedures are not presented as an all-inclusive battery of tests to measure attributes necessary for successful participation in a mobility program, but are merely the beginnings of a more complete battery of perceptual-motor tests which might be devised when more normative data are available. It is hoped that individuals utilizing these tests will supply this investigator with additional data upon which these norms may be revised.

SUMMARY

The administration of two tests was described which were intended to assess two basic perceptual-motor attributes of the blind, important when participating in mobility programs. One evaluates the veering tendency and produces scores, based upon linear deviation after moving approximately 150 feet forward, which determines whether an individual is *good, fair,* or *poor* when attempting to walk a straight line without vision or auditory cues. The second test employs a level riser and two ramps and is an attempt to evaluate the sensitivity of the blind to gradient. These two tasks were developed as starting points in a battery of tests which might evaluate the basic perceptual-motor attributes important to the blind as they participate in programs of mobility training.

The reliability and validity of these tasks, the adjustment of their norms, and the refinement of their administrative techniques are dependent upon the data arising from future investigation. Peripatologists utilizing these tests are encouraged to send this investigator the scores collected as well as suggestions and problems encountered relative to their administration.

REFERENCES

1. Cratty, Bryant J.: Perceptual thresholds of non-visual locomotion. I. The veering tendency, the perception of gradient, and of curvature in pathways: Inter-relationships, norms, inter-group comparisons and a mobility orientation test. Department of Physical Education, University of California at Los Angeles, August 1965.
2. Lund, F. H.: Physical asymmetries and disorientation. *Amer J Psychol*, 42:51, 1930.
3. Rouse, D. L., and Worchel, P.: Veering tendency in the blind. *New Outlook for the Blind*, 49:115, 1955.
4. Schaeffer, A. A.: Spiral movement in man. *J Morph*, 45:293, 1928.

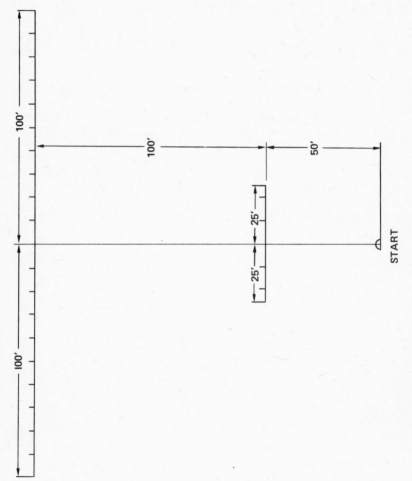

Figure 1. Field layout for measurement of veering tendency.

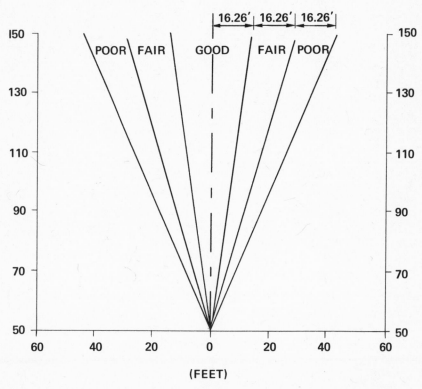

Figure 2. A chart for the assessment of children's veering tendency.

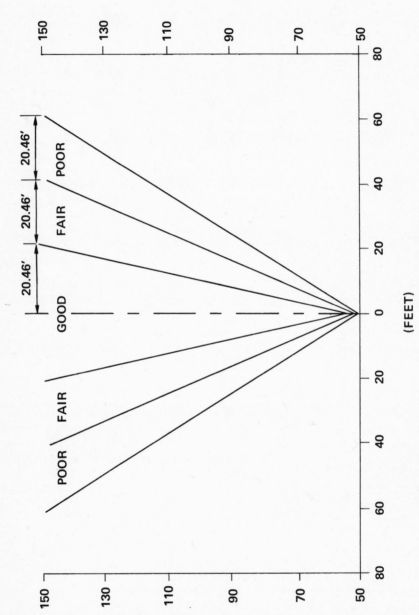

Figure 3. A chart for the assessment of adolescents' veering tendency.

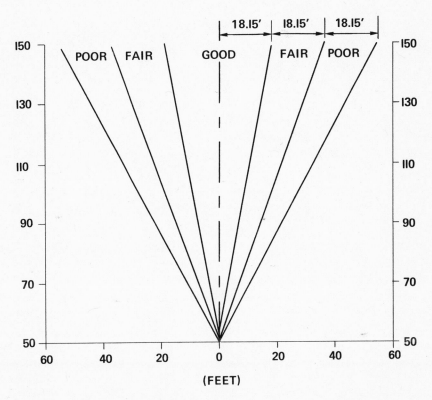

Figure 4. A chart for the assessment of adults' veering tendency.

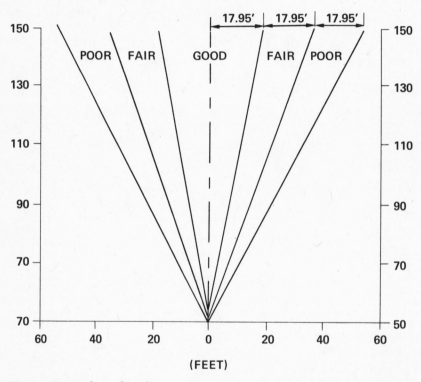

Figure 5. A chart for the assessment of the veering tendency of the
aged.

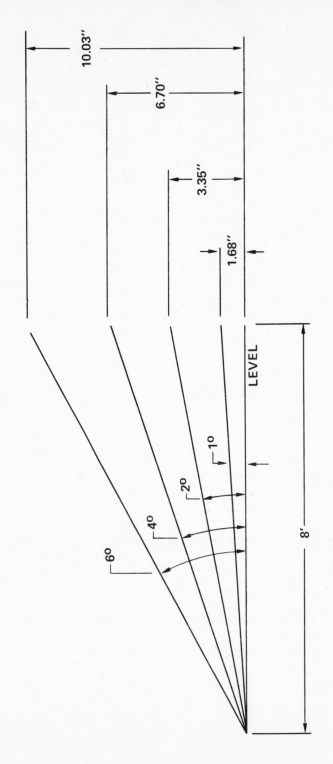

Figure 6. Elevation required at one end of level risers, 8 feet long, to produce 2° of incline.

INDEX